THE

CONVERSION

AND

DEATH-BED EXPERIENCE

OF

MRS. JESSIE LITTLE,

OF GLASGOW,

WHO DIED IN JANUARY, 1842, AT THE AGE OF EIGHTEEN

BY JOHN LITTLE.

FROM THE ELEVENTH LONDON EDITION, REVISED.

PUBLISHED BY THE
AMERICAN TRACT SOCIETY,
150 NASSAU-STREET, NEW YORK.

PREFACE.

The memoir of Mrs. Little being originally written for the private use of her surviving friends, its appearance in public was the result of a repeatedly expressed desire, on the part of a number of esteemed Christian brethren, who were of opinion that its publication might, in the hands of the Spirit, prove useful as an instrument in bringing to peace with God those who were laboring under anxiety regarding their eternal welfare. And it is cheering to record that these anticipations have, in a considerable number of instances, been pleasingly realized.

The edition now published presents the narrative in a revised, and it is hoped a more useful form than it has hitherto possessed.

CONTENTS.

CHAPTER I.

Mrs. Little's first religious impressions—Her want of success as a Sabbath-school teacher—Scripture tests of a true Christian at variance with her experience—Consequent uneasiness about the salvation of her soul—Has recourse to good works—Their failure in bestowing peace—Increasing anxiety about her soul's welfare, ... 7

CHAPTER II.

Attends a prayer-meeting—Finds peace under an address by Mr. Guthrie—New views and feelings—Former misapprehension of the gospel—General difficulties of the unconverted—Review of her past errors in connection with the way of salvation, ... 20

CHAPTER III.

Experience as a believer—Former difficulties—Erroneous ideas regarding "works"—Connection with North Albion-street church—Love to the brethren, to believers in general, and to the world—Sacrifices for the spread of the gospel—Worldly pleasures—Scottish music and sacred poetry, ... 45

CHAPTER IV.

Commencement of her illness—Resignation—Parting with her child—Increasing happiness—The illness and death of her child—Cheerfulness under the trial—Prospect of parting with her husband—Message to her friends—Intense physical suffering—Peace of mind—Consciousness of her safety in Jesus, ... 65

CHAPTER V.

Prayer—Advantages derived from it—Increasing physical sufferings—Their abatement—State of her mind—Jesus the source of her joy—Apparent approach of death—Her consciousness of it—God's promise fulfilled—The love of Christ and her own ingratitude—Message to her medical attendants—The text for her funeral-sermon—Prayer answered—The work of Christ, ... 85

CHAPTER VI.

The approach of death—Interview with Mrs. Campbell—The state of her mind—Spiritual joy—Parting requests—Foretaste of heaven—Her death—Meeting of her acquaintances—Her funeral—Her funeral-sermon—Manuscript written by Mrs. Little, ... 109

MRS. JESSIE LITTLE.

CHAPTER I.

MRS. LITTLE'S FIRST RELIGIOUS IMPRESSIONS—HER WANT OF SUCCESS AS A SABBATH-SCHOOL TEACHER—SCRIPTURE TESTS OF A TRUE CHRISTIAN AT VARIANCE WITH HER EXPERIENCE—CONSEQUENT UNEASINESS ABOUT THE SALVATION OF HER SOUL—HAS RECOURSE TO GOOD WORKS—THEIR FAILURE IN BESTOWING PEACE—INCREASING ANXIETY ABOUT HER SOUL'S WELFARE

ALTHOUGH possessed of what might be considered, for her years, an extensive acquaintance with the divine word, it was not till the year 1839 that any thing like serious impressions appeared on the mind of Mrs. Little, regarding her prospects for eternity. She was then in the fifteenth year of her age, and having been early and suddenly deprived of her father by death, was under the kind guardianship of her uncle, Mr. Cumming of Selkirk. Here she enjoyed, in an eminent degree, advantages favorable to the religious culture of the mind. In her aunt, in whom were developed some of the loveliest features of the

Christian character, she found not only the kindest affection of a mother, but a constant pattern of every thing that was calculated to impress her mind with the reality and value of the religion of Jesus Christ.

About this period, Mrs. Little—then Miss Jessie Cumming—began to be engaged in some of the more active duties which devolve on individual Christians: having for some time been a pupil, she was now considered, from her acquaintance with the Scriptures and her general intelligence, qualified to take a class under her own immediate charge; and consequently became a teacher in the Sabbath-school in connection with the Secession church at Selkirk, under the pastoral charge of Mr. George Lawson. With the Female Religious Tract Society in Selkirk she was also connected, and was personally engaged in the distribution of their useful publications from house to house. To this duty, as well as to those connected with the class in the Sabbath-school, she devoted herself with much assiduity and attention. From the prayer and fellowship meetings, which were held weekly by some of the pious people connected with Mr.

Lawson's church, she was rarely ever found absent; and in short, to appearance, was in every respect diligent and industrious, at all times and seasons, in the service of the Lord and in promoting his cause by all the means that lay within her power. She continued to discharge these and other Christian duties, for a considerable length of time, with a zeal and fidelity, and with a walk and conversation, becoming in every respect to a disciple of the Lord Jesus; while her naturally sweet and unobtrusive disposition, throwing a deeper tinge of humility over all her efforts, tended to strengthen the impression that she was in reality one of those who were "born again;" and thus, not only to an outward observer, but even to her own mind, did she appear to correspond with such a character—at least, if any doubts on the subject ever presented themselves to her attention, they were speedily dispersed before the flow of satisfaction which usually followed the exercise, on her part, of various Christian duties, such as a strict observance of the Lord's day, regularity in her private devotional exercises, and attendance at prayer-meetings.

Under these common, but delusive and dangerous ideas as to what constitutes a child of God, Mrs. Little labored for a considerable period of time. Not very long, however, after the class in the Sabbath-school had been committed to her charge, she felt a conviction growing and deepening on her mind, that her labors in that class were productive of no actual beneficial results, of not even the most distant appearance of any thing like serious impressions on the minds of the children; she failed to make them *sedate* and *serious*, which was probably all she was endeavoring to effect. This state of matters in her class was to her mind a source of much grief and pain, and produced considerable reflection on the subject, and on various means for securing to her efforts a larger degree of success. At length she began to pray more frequently and more earnestly, that her labors might be more blessed, and her dealings with young immortal souls more successful, at the same time renewing her exertions with increased vigor, lest the Lord might call her an unprofitable servant. Still, however, no satisfactory evidence was given by any of the children, that the great truths she was constantly endeavoring to bring before their minds were at all interesting them, or producing more than ordinary attention: her many prayers and increased exertions all appeared to be expended in vain, and the only considerations which induced her to continue her labors, were the hope that the seed she was now endeavoring to sow might be watered by the Lord, and hereafter spring up to his praise and glory; and also the conviction that she was discharging, to the utmost of her ability, those duties for the due performance of which she considered that the many privileges which she, as a Christian, enjoyed, rendered her responsible; cherishing at the same time the false and delusive idea, that if her labors were not blessed here, the performance of them on her part would at least meet with due reward on the part of God hereafter. Such ideas yielded her—as, to nominal professors, they often do—a false peace and satisfaction for the present, and presented a somewhat plausible appearance of encouragement for the future—motives which possessed strength enough to induce her still to persevere in her labors, although any thing like success or the realization of her wishes appeared to be as far distant as ever.

About this time, also, another source of pain and perplexity, but of a far deeper and more distressing character, made its appearance on her mind. A careful perusal of the inspired volume discovered to her the fact, that the true people of God enjoy a peace of mind which takes away the fear of death—a peace which the world can neither give nor take away—a peace which "passeth all understanding;" while at the same time she found that her own conscience and experience by no means corresponded with any such declarations: on the contrary, on instituting a calm and faithful examination of her own heart, she found that the sting of death was *not* taken away, that the perishing things of this world formed the source from which she derived her chief enjoyments, and that her small measure of spiritual peace was created by the performance of certain duties on her part, and not by the conveyance to her mind of a certain truth contained in the Bible, or by the knowledge of a work already finished and completed on the part of Jesus, as revealed in the Scriptures.

Under such a scrutiny, it may easily be conceived that Mrs. Little's mind derived any thing but satisfaction from her past Christian history, or encouragement from the solemn contemplation of the future; and she now proceeded to reason with herself in the following manner: "The word of God informs me that the believer, even in this life, enjoys a peace of mind which the world can neither give nor take away. 'Peace I leave with you; my peace I give unto you. Not as the world giveth, give I unto you.' On carefully looking into my own heart, I find that I do not possess any such state of mind; consequently the word of God declares *one* thing, and my conscience declares *another: both* cannot be consistent with truth; either the Bible must declare what is not true, or I am not a child of God. But, in all it declares, I believe the Bible to be true; therefore I am yet unsaved, and on the way to eternal woe. Again, the Scriptures also declare that the unbeliever has no peace with God, nor rest for his soul. 'There is no peace, saith my God, to the wicked.' Now I find that I have no real peace of mind, and my soul can find no satisfactory resting-place ; the unavoidable conclusion therefore again is, that I am still an unbeliever, 'without God and without hope in the world.'" And further, in breaking through the merely external habiliments of her Christian profession, and going down to the secret recesses of her own heart, dragging out her whole motives, and laying them bare and naked before the searching and analyzing eye of a rigid and impartial conscience, she found that the elements of which her religion was composed consisted of nothing more than a dread of future punishment, a desire for her own future safety and happiness, and lastly, of an extensive round of Christian duties, as the means for protecting her against eternal death and for securing to her soul the possession of eternal life.

Such was, at this period, the sum and substance of Mrs. Little's Christianity—such the composition of the structure upon which her immortal soul was resting its hopes for eternity. Is this the Rock of ages, or is it not? was now the all-important question; and the Bible being the only standard of truth, was alone competent to present her with a satisfactory reply. But a further examination of the sacred volume conveyed to her mind no intimation that the religion of Jesus Christ consisted either in a dread of future punishment, or in a desire for future safety and happiness; and nowhere could she find it mentioned, that the mere observance of certain external Christian duties secured the eternal welfare of the soul. The inevitable conclusion, therefore, at which her mind arrived, was, that she was still an unconverted sinner, unsaved, and in danger every moment of dropping into eternity, to endure the wrath and curse of God for ever and ever; and, so far as all her former good works and exertions in the cause of Christ were concerned, she now saw that they were in themselves no way calculated to introduce her into the everlasting fellowship of a perfectly holy Being whose laws she had violated; but were, on the contrary, an abomination in the sight of the Lord, only fitting her for condemnation, instead of qualifying her, as she had hitherto imagined, for the reception of God's favor and love.

These were new and most alarming announcements, but which the conclusion of every faithful and impartial debate with her own conscience, of every examination into her own heart, and of every appeal to the sacred volume on the subject of her soul's eternal welfare, only served to confirm. From without, the word of God exclaimed, "Unsaved! unsaved!" and from within, conscience echoed back the dismal sound, "Unsaved! unsaved!" evidence which was conclusive to her own mind in establishing the melancholy fact, that she was really and truly an unbeliever, and consequently in momentary danger of eternally losing her soul.

This truth being thus established on what she considered the most indubitable evidence, she proceeded to follow out its results in the subsequent stages of her disagreeable and humbling argument, in substance, as follows: "Now the Bible further declares, that none but believers can inherit the kingdom of God. 'Believe in the Lord Jesus Christ, and thou shalt be saved; believe not, and thou shalt be damned.' I am not a believer; therefore I cannot inherit that kingdom. The soul of an unbeliever is in jeopardy every moment of being lost for ever; my soul, therefore, is in momentary danger of eternal destruction. Thousands and tens of thousands are hurried into eternity without a moment's notice; and why may not I be? My dear father was found, to our sad and melancholy surprise, one morning stretched in his bed a cold and lifeless corpse; and why may it not be thus with me to-morrow morning?"

In this, and in other ways, she continued for some time to reason with herself, and the result of every such argument only tended to deepen the deplorable conviction that she was a lost sinner, posting onward with fearful rapidity to the depths of destruction, and liable to be plunged into that awful pit of misery where the wrath of God burneth for ever and ever, to mingle her cries with the eternal wail of the lost. Her only resource now lay in the hope, that the Lord might still permit her to remain in the land of the living, till she attained possession of that peace which is the result of genuine faith in the Son of God, and a consciousness of pardon through the merits of his atonement; and for this purpose, strange to say, instead of going direct to the word of Him who "cannot lie," and simply receiving the good news which the Holy Spirit had there to communicate, namely, that the very thing which alone could convey peace to her mind here, and procure salvation to her soul hereafter, was *already* done—that Jesus had *already* died to "take away the sin of the world," that he had finished the work of atonement—she now put into energetic practice the cultivation of pious and holy thoughts and feelings, great purity in life, and other similar exercises, at the same time constantly looking *in* to her own heart, and watching with anxiety every movement of her mind for the appearance of faith; or in other words, for that peace, the consequence of genuine faith, which she had so much desired—exercises which, though mental and internal, the believing reader will at once perceive, still resolved themselves into a kind of meritorious works or righteousness of her own, and consequently were just as worthless for effecting the end she had in view as the more external observances in which she had formerly been in the habit of engaging.

Under the employment of these vain and futile efforts to obtain possession of faith, it is needless to observe, she did not effect the object of her wishes. In this somewhat perplexed condition she continued for a considerable number of weeks, revealing to no one the real state of her mind; but, on the contrary, maintaining a careful concealment of the difficulties with which she felt herself to be surrounded; and, being considered by all her friends and acquaintances as a most pious and amiable girl, and much beloved on account of her sweet and engaging disposition, no one appeared to entertain the suspicion that she was really that which her own conscience told her she was—a poor, rebellious, unpardoned sinner, virtually "without God and without hope in the world;" in plain and solemn language, an infidel: for however high his or her moral character may stand in the estimation of man, an unbeliever stands in the eye of God on exactly the same level as the man who does not acknowledge a God; "For whosoever denieth the Son, hath not the Father." Such were her convictions, notwithstanding all her endeavors to love and to do the will of God.

CHAPTER II.

ATTENDS A PRAYER-MEETING—FINDS PEACE UNDER AN ADDRESS BY MR. GUTHRIE—NEW VIEWS AND FEELINGS—FORMER MISAPPREHENSION OF THE GOSPEL—GENERAL DIFFICULTIES OF THE UNCONVERTED—REVIEW OF HER PAST ERRORS IN CONNECTION WITH THE WAY OF SALVATION.

MRS. LITTLE was in this state of mind when, in the providence of God, information reached her one day that a small meeting for prayer and other spiritual exercises was to be held in the evening, at which Mr. John Guthrie, a Christian brother from Jedburgh, was to be present and to favor the meeting with a short address. As was her custom on such occasions, Mrs. Little made it a point of duty to attend, and was consequently among the number present at the meeting. The words which formed the subject of Mr. Guthrie's address were those in the fifteenth verse of the eighty-ninth Psalm: "Blessed is the people that know the joyful sound." In his remarks, Mr. Guthrie pointed out in a clear and simple manner the way of salvation through faith in the Son of God; showing the intimate and natural connection between the belief of the truth as it is in Jesus, and the peace which the mind enjoys under that belief; proving that the one was a necessary consequence of the other, and stating in other respects how "blessed is the people that know the joyful sound."

The address was illustrated in the most homely and simple, but pointed manner; and was entirely free from all that metaphysical language, which, when employed in connection with the statement of the simple saving truth tends so much to bewilder the poor anxious inquirer to Zion—trembling, perhaps, on the brink of eternity—and to throw up mist between the eye of his mind and the short and simple story of the cross, the reception of which brings the soul into the possession of peace and the enjoyment of salvation. In short, so exactly did Mr. Guthrie's remarks apply to her own peculiar state of mind at the time, and so faithfully was her true character portrayed, that she felt almost inclined to believe that the address had been composed under the knowledge of, and with a view of meeting her own individual case. The consequence was, that Mr. Guthrie's faithful and simple remarks were the means, in the hands of the Holy Spirit, of winning her soul into delightful contact with the "joyful sound," that is, with the *gospel*, or in other words, with *the truth about Jesus;* which gospel or truth about Jesus exhibited to her mind the fact, that God had "so loved" her that he had given his only and beloved Son, "who bore her sins in his own body on the tree;" and consequently that Jesus, by thus suffering in her room, had rendered a full and perfect reparation to that divine law which she had violated; and also that God, as the righteous executor of that law, was now as completely pleased with and reconciled to her, on account of what Jesus had done, as if no sin and no violation of his law whatever had on her part been committed.

But while, through the medium of the gospel, the atonement of Jesus thus presented itself to her mind as a propitiation or satisfaction, of the most perfect and complete character, to God for every sin; at the same time, that very perfection which that propitiation exhibited produced, as a necessary consequence, the destruction of all those hopes in herself, or in her own good works, which she had hitherto been, to a greater or less extent, in the habit of cherishing; and thus, as the weary bird of passage, after vainly attempting to seek repose on the restless wave, reaches the land and rests with conscious safety, so, after vainly endeavoring to rest her soul on the unstable and perishing works of her own creation, she laid her spirit down, "weary and heavy laden," on the finished work of the Son of God, and immediately found rest and consciousness of safety; for this is "the Rock of ages," "the same yesterday, to-day, and for ever." In more simple terms, she was informed by the gospel, dictated by the unerring Spirit, that the very object, namely, a propitiation to God for her sins, which she had hitherto been vainly endeavoring to create, was already fully and perfectly accomplished by Jesus Christ more than eighteen hundred years before; and the consequence was, that she returned home from that meeting with the eye of her soul turned away from searching *within* her own sinful heart for grounds of acceptance, and directed to the sinless sacrifice *without*—away from her own imperfect doings to the *perfect* work of Jesus, and rejoicing as if her mind had been relieved from the pressure of a heavy burden. In short, she was a new creature; old things now began to pass away, and all things became new.

Thus Mrs. Little's spiritual chains were broken—thus she entered into the liberty of the gospel; and as she now stood calmly looking around, and solemnly reviewing, under the sunshine of divine truth, the position which she had hitherto occupied in the eyes of God, the spectacle which her former religious profession presented to her mind was of the most humbling description; while at the same time the secret of all the doubts and fears and perplexities under which she had formerly labored, and the rocks upon which she had so often stumbled, lay stretched out before her in the light of open day. To dethrone Jesus Christ, to rob him of his glory, to conceal him from her mind, and to attempt to procure salvation independently of Him who is "the way, the truth, and the life," and by a way of her own—that is, by her doing some work without her, or creating some good thing within her—Mrs. Little found was the dangerous principle upon which she had been hitherto unconsciously acting, and to the continued operation of which may be ascribed her real difficulties, in entering into the rest and liberty of the children of God by faith in Jesus.

For the benefit of the unconverted reader, and the anxious inquirer who may be laboring under the same state of mind, and harboring his soul under the same false refuges, it may not perhaps be out of place to dwell somewhat minutely upon those principles on which she acted previous to her knowing the truth—previous to her making the work of Jesus *the* ground, and the *only* ground of her hopes—and which will be found operating, to a greater or less extent, in the case of the great majority of those who are laboring under anxiety regarding the all-important subject of their soul's eternal safety.

The great inquiry which has proceeded from anxious sinners in all ages, has been, "What shall I do to be saved?" to which the words of God, "Believe on the Lord Jesus Christ, and thou shalt be saved," form the simple and everlasting reply. The practical application of this simple requirement here laid down by God appears, however, either to have been misunderstood by Mrs. Little, or which amounts to the same thing, to have been associated in her mind with the employment on her part, of certain means which, in their operation, exhibited both directly and indirectly the existence of quite a different principle from the one contained in the word of God already quoted, and which, instead of leading her soul to "believe on the Lord Jesus Christ and be saved," encouraged the formation and nourishment of a system under which many souls are kept in bondage, and, it is feared, finally ruined. The leading error here alluded to generally makes its appearance under three slightly different aspects:

1. In the employment, on the part of the unconverted sinner, of *various Christian duties as the ground of his hopes for eternity*. This form of the error is correctly illustrated in a case which came under the observation of the writer, of an aged woman who applied for fellowship with a Christian church in Glasgow. After being informed that the purity and consequent usefulness of the church, as well as duty to the applicants' own souls, required, on the part of the church, the exercise of great

and affectionate fidelity in the admission of its members, she was requested to furnish the church, as was usual on such occasions, with the grounds upon which she rested her qualifications of membership with a company of believers. Without any hesitation, she proceeded to relate, that from her youth she had been considered very exemplary, had never been accustomed to mix with loose and indifferent company, never told a lie, was regular in all her devotional exercises, took great delight in reading the word of God, and besides, had for a considerable number of years been a member of a Christian church. She was affectionately informed, that although what she had mentioned were not only the duties but the privileges of every child of God, yet the mere observance of these duties did not *constitute* a Christian—that the ground of the believer's confidence was composed of something very different from any thing to which she had alluded, and that it was eternal, "the same yesterday, to-day, and for ever;" whereas these observances commenced with the sinner, and would end with his existence on earth. On further conversation with this poor woman, who appeared to be upwards of "threescore years and ten," it was found that the Lamb of God had never been permitted to take possession of her affections; that Christ crucified had never formed the pillar of her hopes for eternity; and that for more than fifty years she had, in perfect self-complacency, been resting her precious soul on no other foundation than her own perishing works. Of course the church, under the circumstances, could do nothing more than endeavor affectionately to lead her to Him, than by whom "there is *no other way*" by which she could see the kingdom of God.

Under the operation of the same dangerous principles with the woman above alluded to, Mrs. Little's practical profession of Christianity, in the first stage of its existence, appears to have been conducted—principles which in theory, it is true, recognize Jesus, but which in reality produce a rejection of Him "who is the way, the truth, and the life." Thus her error consisted in seeking salvation on the ground of works executed by *herself*, instead of receiving it as a *gift* through the work finished by *Jesus*. As the tradesman points to the execution of the work with which he is intrusted as his claim for remuneration, so, as a ground of pardon, she was directing God to the performance on her part of certain duties which, as a ground of justification, are an abomination in his sight, instead of presenting him with the work of his own Son as the only foundation of her hope—a work with which God is ever well pleased, with which alone divine justice is ever satisfied. In short, she found that she had been virtually presenting to God with the one hand her prayers, her tears, and her good works, as a price for her redemption, and stretching out the other to receive salvation in exchange; while the patient, and long-suffering, but insulted Jehovah, who "takes no pleasure in the death of the wicked," was through his word proclaiming in her ear, "To what purpose is the multitude of your sacrifices to me? Bring no more vain oblations, they are a trouble unto me; I am weary to bear them." "Wherefore do you spend money for that which is not bread, and your labor for that which satisfieth not?" Only "believe on the Lord Jesus Christ, and thou shalt be saved." In plain human language, it is not only of not the most remote advantage, but, on the contrary, an actual grieving and mocking of Him "who willeth all men to be saved," for you, unconverted sinner, to do any work, however good or great it may be, for the purpose of laying a foundation for, or meriting the salvation of your soul, and just for the simple and palpable reason that the work—on account of which alone the gates of heaven are now open to the very chief of sinners—is already finished by Jesus, for "the sin of the world," and therefore for yours; and with which finished work God your judge exclaims, "I am well pleased," and his law, which you violated, "I am satisfied." Be you then also well pleased and satisfied with the same finished work as a complete atonement for your sins, and your name is "Believer."

Thus the first branch of the system of error under which Mrs. Little labored, consisted in virtually overlooking the only ground which is capable of affording peace to the soul, namely, the merits of Jesus, and seeking salvation through the medium of her own works.

2. The second description of mistaken views of God's plan of salvation, which appears to have surrounded Mrs. Little with not a few difficulties, and to have formed a very power-

ful barrier between her mind and the simple truth about Jesus, or the "good news," was the endeavoring on her part *to obtain or produce faith by the same means*, that is, by the employment on her part of various exercises of an operative nature—an error which is found expressed in the question so frequently employed by the anxious inquirer, "But how am I to believe?" or, as it is sometimes expressed, "How am I to obtain peace, that is, the peace of the gospel?" That the gospel produces, in the mind of the individual believing it, a peculiar peace and joy, the experience of every renewed soul can testify; but *how* or *why* it does so, every believer can equally testify is just simply because the gospel, the thing believed, is "good news," is tidings of "great joy."

To bring this fact more clearly before the mind of the unconverted but inquiring reader, advantage may here be taken of a simple illustration. An affectionate wife is presented with a letter, conveying to her the information that her absent husband has safely arrived in port, after a long and dangerous voyage, and that in a few hours he will be in the midst of his little family circle. The bosom of that wife beats with joy, and the countenances of her little ones beam with delight at the joyful news of their father's return. Enter yon other dwelling. There too is a fond wife, but she is in tears; there too is a sweet little family, but their little hearts are ready to break, as they stand sobbing around their weeping mother. She too had been presented that morning with a letter—she too had a loving spouse on the stormy sea. But no happy meeting awaited her. The object of her affections, and the father of her little ones, was never again to return; the form on which her eyes delighted to dwell was a cold and lifeless corpse, tossing in the watery deep. Thus are two states of mind produced of entirely opposite character; the one a state of great joy, the other of extreme sorrow: but *how* are they produced? evidently by the employment neither of external means nor of internal or mental efforts; but simply and solely by the *nature* of the respective truths, or "news," or "tidings" presented before the minds of the two respective parties. Thus, joy is produced by joyful news, and sorrow by sorrowful tidings.

Again, suppose that on the morning of his

execution, the cell of an unhappy man who has been taken prisoner in the act of unjustly invading a friendly territory, and condemned to die, is entered by a messenger announcing that a ransom has been paid and accepted by the king of the invaded country, for his immediate pardon; the moment the intelligence comes in contact with the mind of the criminal, that moment the flash of delight reddens his pale countenance. In like manner, the gospel is the communication from God to man—through the medium of the Bible, the Holy Spirit's word—of one of the most extraordinary and soul-cheering truths that could be presented to the attention of an immortal mind: namely, that God so loved the sinner, that to prevent him from perishing for ever, and to bring him into the possession of eternal felicity, his sins, which formed the only barrier between his soul and the enjoyment of that felicity, have been atoned for and borne away; thereby leaving the eye of Jehovah looking down through that atonement on the sinner as if he had never sinned. In other words, God looks on the sinner through the medium of Christ's righteousness, and is well pleased, or reconciled, for that righteousness' sake. The necessary and natural effect, then, on the mind of that sinner who simply receives the gospel announcement as a truth, or, which amounts to the same thing, is reconciled to God by the *same work* which reconciles God to him, is at once the possession of a sense of safety, and a peace with God which "the world can neither give nor take away."

But the very proposal of such a question as the one referred to, by the inquirer, leaves behind it palpable evidence, that in solving it for himself he is calling into operation a principle directly opposed to every thing like reason, by looking for a consequence without a cause; that is, in endeavoring to obtain peace for his soul, his attention is evidently directed not to the truth about Jesus, which is the *producer*, but to his own mind, which is simply the *receiver* of that peace. The peace of the gospel being *in the gospel*, any attempt on the part of the inquirer to extract peace either from the performance of external works or from his own bosom, where there is nothing but sin, will be as unsuccessful as the search in the field for a watch which was lost in the garden.

Under this very common but radical error, Mrs. Little, as has been mentioned, labored for some time, making "*How* shall I believe?" instead of "*What* shall I believe?" her inquiry, and *faith*, instead of *the truth about Christ*, the object of her investigations, tormenting herself about the *act* of believing, and at the same time shutting her eyes on the *object* to be believed; and consequently, she had been constantly directing her attention inward to the movements of her own mind, instead of outward to a crucified Saviour—endeavoring rather to produce peace with God from the materials within her own bosom, than to receive it by a simple knowledge from the Holy Spirit's testimony of what had been done by Jesus for her. Her efforts to obtain faith through the practice of works of a more formal and external nature, were of course equally unsuccessful, for the same reason, that these in themselves did not compose the *object of faith*.

To the instructions contained in the Holy Spirit's word, and to the ingress to the mind of the truth which "saves and sets the sinner free," two forms of opposition, it will be observed, have already been mentioned as making their appearance in the mind and practice of Mrs. Little: first, in seeking *salvation* through the exercise of various external and internal duties; second, in seeking *faith* through the operation of similar means.

3. Intimately connected with these erroneous views of divine truth, which inquirers are apt to cherish, was another, from which Mrs. Little did not entirely escape; and which, for the sake of the unconverted reader, it may not perhaps be considered superfluous briefly to notice, as it tends to draw the attention away from saving truth to the employment of self-righteous means in endeavoring to obtain possession of that truth. I allude to the impression frequently found lodged in the mind of an awakened sinner, that although God is willing to receive him through Christ, he—the sinner—has still something to do, some little work to perform, *some preparatory purifying process of the heart* to go through, *before* trusting to Christ; employing such reasoning as the following, in support of his position: "I am so sinful, my heart is so cold and wicked, and I have lived such a careless, prayerless life, that it would be presumption in me to expect pardon in my

present state. I shall first endeavor to get quit of my coldness and sinfulness of heart, and otherwise become better, and then I shall be able to look up to God for pardon with these feelings of presumption somewhat abated." Such language has all the appearance of humility, and is sometimes called by that name: under a very slight glance, however, it will be found to be only a plausible method of deceiving the sinner's own soul—of dishonoring God and the finished work of his Son: in plain and honest terms, it means, "I am not satisfied with the work of Christ; it is not sufficient in itself to meet divine justice; it is not true that God is 'well pleased' with the work of Christ for my sins; it is not true that 'the blood of Jesus cleanseth from *all* sin;' I must, therefore, myself make up for what is deficient in the atonement of the Son of God—I must first reach a standard of righteousness at which my sins will appear so trifling, that the work of Christ will then, perhaps, be able to atone for them." Now, it is quite true that the sinner is unworthy, and that, too, to an extent inconceivably beyond that to which he is now confessing. Nay, could he get a view of his own heart as

God sees it, the awful spectacle would probably deprive him of his reason. He can acquire a knowledge of the heinous character of sin in the eyes of a holy God, only from the fact, that to atone or make reparation to God's laws for that sin, the sacrifice of a man, or of an angel, or even of an archangel, was not enough—that nothing less than the crucifying of *the divine Redeemer* was sufficient; and he may also be provided with a perfect security of the completeness and God-satisfying character of Christ's atonement, by the same wonderful fact, that it was not a man, nor an angel, nor even an archangel, who was the atoner, or who formed the atoning sacrifice, but the second person in the Trinity united with man. In short, it was God himself who required the satisfaction or atonement, and it was God himself who made the satisfaction or atonement. God himself, as a just Being, demanded the performance of a work, and God himself executed that work; and if that work, as an atonement for sin, be insufficient to satisfy God, then God's own work is insufficient to satify himself. But God's works are all perfect; and the atonement made for sin is God's work; therefore the atonement made for sin is in itself perfect and complete.

Thus neither, on the one hand, does the great number of the sinner's past transgressions militate against the perfect sufficiency of Christ's atonement to meet his peculiar and aggravated case, or their magnitude overtop the burning love of Jehovah to his soul; nor, on the other hand, does the numerous array of good actions, or the small number of bad ones, on the part of the sinner, constitute, in the very least degree, any of the ground upon which he can rest his hopes for eternity. No; the ground of safety exhibits itself to the mind of the sinner from a point outside of himself, outside of his works, outside of his feelings, outside of his prayers, outside of even his faith: it makes its appearance only in Jesus. Eternal life is a gift, something given on the part of God, and that gift is entirely concentrated and encased in his own Son. Hopes, therefore, which have their foundation out of Jesus, are false hopes—and the sinner's works, and feelings, and prayers, and faith, are all things which are out of Jesus; therefore, hopes of salvation springing out of or resting on works, or feelings, or prayers, or faith, on the part of the sinner, are false and delusive; and hence, in the same proportion as the sinner, in his anxiety for the possession of peace with God, presses his own works, however excellent these in themselves may be, into the notice of the divine Being, as forming either by themselves or in conjunction with the work of Christ, the foundation of his hopes for eternity, does he dishonor and distrust the perfect atonement of the Son of God, and consequently to the same extent rears barriers between his own soul and the enjoyment of eternal life.

Of the practical influence of these principles, Mrs. Little, as has already been mentioned, was to a certain extent a subject. She found that her hopes of the future well-being of her soul rested on two foundations: first, the work performed by Jesus, and secondly, the works performed by herself. The latter were intended to counterbalance any want of confidence which her mind might manifest in the former. Under such circumstances, her soul did not and could not enter into possession of that "peace which passeth understanding," whose whole being is derived from and exists on the finished atonement of Jesus, and that *alone.*

Illustrative of this principle of amalgamating the work of Christ with that of the sinner, as conjointly forming the ground of salvation, a case in point may be mentioned, which fell under my own observation. Some time ago, in Ireland, I met with an interesting and intelligent Catholic lady. It was on a Friday, a day on which, the reader will be aware, the church of Rome enjoins her members to abstain from the use of meat; and at dinner, true to her principles, she did not partake of this kind of food, a circumstance which led us into a friendly and interesting conversation on what constituted the true ground of a sinner's hope for eternity. With a view of discovering exactly the genuine character of the elements which composed the foundation on which she, as a Catholic, rested her hopes of salvation, I kindly requested her to permit her mind to arrange before it all her bygone fasts, mass observances, penances, and all the other rites and ceremonies of the church with which she was connected, together with all her pious feelings, and every good word and deed which she had ever said or done; and then to suppose the whole, in one sweep, borne away out of her view and annihilated for ever. Would she, it was then asked, under such circumstances, feel the ground of her hopes for eternity any way shaken or destroyed? "Most decidedly I would," the lady with the utmost candor replied: an answer which does not require the employment of any argument to establish the fact, that she was not only calling in question the work of Christ, as a sufficient and complete atonement for all the sins with which she was chargeable, suspecting the truthfulness of God's own statement that he was "well pleased," for Christ's righteousness' sake, and the verity of his own comforting declaration, that "the blood of Jesus Christ cleanseth from all sin;" but that she was clinging to a position, the continued and determined occupation of which *necessarily* issues in the eternal ruin of the soul. For as no progress can be made by the traveller to the top of the tall and towering dome, while only one foot is placed on the steps which lead to its lofty summit, the other still resting on the ground; so the sinner can never make one step of heavenward advancement, while only one foot is placed on Jesus, who is "the ladder to glory," and the other still rests on the earth, which is his own works. And as the mariner can never reach his destination on the far and foreign shore, without first stepping off the beach of his native land and committing his whole body to the vessel which is to bear him across the billowy deep; so the sinner can never traverse the ocean of sin, and land on the happy shores of the heavenly country, unless he first step off, completely off the sand-bank of his own works, and commit his soul fully and wholly to the work of Christ, which is the secure and danger-proof ark that will carry him calmly and safely to the haven of eternal rest: and further, as every stone of the building must fall to the earth, when the swelling waves shall wash away the heap of sand which formed its frail foundation; so *every* hope resting on works executed out of Jesus, and *by* the sinner, *must* perish when death shall sweep away for ever these works themselves. Perhaps the reader may at present be in a somewhat similar position; for it is one which is by no means confined to that portion of our fellow-men who compose the Romish church; and if so, he may rest assured that, like the subject of this memoir at this stage of her experience, he is "spending his money for that which is not bread, and his labor for that which satisfieth not:" the work which forms the sole and only ground of salvation being, as already mentioned, entirely out of and separate from his works, and entirely in *Jesus*, that is, in the work executed by Jesus for the sinner.

CHAPTER III.

EXPERIENCE AS A BELIEVER—FORMER DIFFICULTIES—ERRONEOUS IDEAS REGARDING "WORKS"—CONNECTION WITH NORTH-ALBION-STREET CHURCH—LOVE TO THE BRETHREN, TO BELIEVERS IN GENERAL, AND TO THE WORLD—SACRIFICES FOR THE SPREAD OF THE GOSPEL—WORLDLY PLEASURES—SCOTTISH MUSIC AND SACRED POETRY.

SUCH were some of the more prominent features which characterized the latter part of the period of Mrs. Little's nominal profession of the religion of Jesus Christ. Her experience as a genuine professor, as a true believer, may now be briefly considered. Not very long ago the writer of these pages heard from the lips of a young man, a converted Roman Catholic, in the north of Ireland, the statement, that when in connection with the church of Rome, he was, with the view of atoning for his sins, in the habit of proceeding in the cold and stormy nights of winter to the fields, of there embedding his naked knees in the freezing mounds of snow, and in that position remaining for several hours together; also, that for three months successively, in every year, he would not permit himself to partake of more than one meal in twenty-four hours; and further, that he would annually make a pilgrimage to the grave of St. Patrick, more than forty miles distant, walking a portion of the way on his uncovered knees, bleeding and lacerated as they were; and that in a great variety of ways he would inflict upon himself severe physical punishment, for the purpose of atoning to God for his violation of divine laws. At length he was, with great difficulty, prevailed upon one evening to accompany a Protestant gentleman to the place of worship with which the latter was connected, for the purpose of hearing a sermon which was there to be preached by a worthy and devoted minister in connection with the Irish Presbyterian church. The words which formed the subject of the minister's address were, "The blood of Jesus Christ his Son cleanseth us from all sin." After sitting for some time under a feeling of considerable uneasiness at the idea of his being located in the midst of Protestant people, and in a Protestant place of worship, the hitherto zealous and devoted Catholic began to be somewhat interested. The doctrine that the blood of Jesus of *itself* could atone to God for *all* sin, was one with which his mind had not previously formed an acquaintance; for although he was somewhat advanced in classical attainments and general literature, and intended by his friends for the priesthood in connection with the Romish church, yet the Bible had, up to this period, been to him as a book that was sealed. The consequence was, that the words sounded like "*good news*" in his ear, the expression had a "*joyful* sound" in it; "for if," said he to himself, "if the blood of Jesus of itself is capable of cleansing from *all* sin, and rendering a full satisfaction to the violated laws of God, for what purpose are all those harassing and physically distressing observances which I force myself to undergo, and under which my very body groans, in order to unburden my soul of its guilt? Truly this is a simple method of salvation indeed." Before the worthy servant of God had concluded his address, the sincere but work-bound Catholic saw, to his amazement and delight, that the whole work needful for the sinner's salvation was already done, already finished by Jesus: he believed it, because it was the word of Him who "cannot lie;" and believing it, he was saved, for "he that believeth hath eternal life;" and being saved, an entirely new principle took possession of his soul—a principle which conducted him more energetically than ever to the performance of Christian works and duties: but, instead of betaking himself to the fields, to expose his body to the inclemency of the weather—instead of maltreating himself, and refusing the demands of nature by depriving his body of its nourishment, as acts of atonement for his sins—he now went about from house to house proclaiming to his unconverted friends and acquaintances, that "the blood of Jesus cleanseth from *all* sin;" that the work of atonement was not the sinner's, but the Saviour's work; and that the sinner was saved, not by doing something himself, but simply by trusting in something already done by Jesus.

Thus it was with Mrs. Little. As soon as her mind perceived that salvation was to be found solely in the work of Christ, and that that work itself had satisfied God, itself continued to satisfy God, and would itself for ever continue to satisfy God for all her sins, she found peace, and the establishment in her mind of a principle which completely reversed her whole former practice. The work of salvation had been hitherto always connected in her mind with the idea of something being done by herself; now she saw that the whole meritorious work was already done, and done by another. Formerly, she strove to make works produce faith; now, her faith produced works. Before, she looked inward to her own heart for peace, but found it not; now, she looked outward, and away to "the Lamb of God who taketh away the sins of the world," and peace and joy were the immediate consequence. Hitherto she had been laboring for the production of good feelings, to make herself a fit subject to receive the truth about Jesus; she now saw that the only qualification necessary for that purpose was to be a sinner—"Christ came not to call the righteous, but sinners," and that qualification she had of course always possessed. Formerly, her heart was cold and selfish, and anxious only for her own salvation; now, it burned with love, and panted for nothing less than the salvation of the world. Formerly, she was unhappy and afraid to die; now, she was full of joy, and the sting of death was taken away.

Allusion has already been made to the small degree of success, and of benefit to the children, which attended the labors of Mrs. Little in connection with the Sabbath-school. What she considered to be the main secret of her failure in this respect, now likewise became evident to her mind: she found that she had been attempting to guide the children under her charge to God by a way to which she herself was a stranger; and that she had been endeavoring to impress on their minds truths which had never been practically admitted by her own. She felt deeply her own inconsistency and sin, in that, while she was taking upon herself the solemn responsibility of a teacher of young immortal souls, candidates for heaven, she was at the same time in the service of Satan and sin herself; and while recommending the acceptance of Jesus to others with her lips, all the while refusing him admission to her own bosom.

Some time after our matrimonial connection, which took place at the close of 1840, we were led, in the providence of God, to connect ourselves with the Congregational church assembling in North-Albion-street, under the pastoral care of Rev. Thomas Pullar. There her knowledge of divine truth was greatly enlarged, and, as she termed it, her heart was always kept warm; "for," said she, "there is always so much of Christ and the cross in his [Mr. Pullar's] sermons." She always contemplated her connection with that church with feelings of peculiar delight; and to the Sabbath-day when she was to meet with her fellow-believers in the chapel, she looked forward with great pleasure and interest, and great was the privation, if circumstances prevented her from attending even a single meeting of the solemn assembly. Her love to the brethren was of a peculiarly fervent character: when one sorrowed she sorrowed, and when one rejoiced she rejoiced, knowing that all were one in Christ Jesus; and even when stretched on the thorny bed of affliction, with the curtains of death closing around her, when she was no more able to mingle among them, to join her voice of praise with theirs, and to sit down with them to commemorate the death of her Lord, she would often make the most affec tionate inquiries regarding all whom she could remember of her "dear brothers and sisters in Jesus;" and of Mr. Pullar she would say, "Oh, I love him for his work's sake." Knowing that in a few short years at most, their various pilgrimages would cease, that the grave would soon close around them, and that the dark valley of the shadow of death would ere long be left behind, she contemplated with great delight the time when they would all again meet in the land of glory, never, never again to part; where sighing and sorrow have for ever fled away; and when they would see Jesus face to face, and be with him for ever.

"Together to their Father's house,
With joyful hearts they go,
And dwell for ever with the Lord,
Beyond the reach of woe.

A few short years of evil past,
We reach the happy shore;
There death-divided friends at last
Shall meet to part no more."

Nor was her love to the brethren confined within mere denominational limits; it was far too extensive, far too pure and exalted to be so circumscribed; and the question with her was not, to what sect of Christians do you belong; what are your views on this point, and on that—this doctrine, or that doctrine—this form of church government, or that; but, "Do you belong to Jesus? What are your views of *Him?* Have you found a Saviour in him? Has your soul found peace in his blood? Has your heart been melted by his love? Has it been changed by his truth? Has it been renewed by his Spirit? If so, we are one—one in Jesus; and, if one in him, then are we one in heart, one in spirit, of one family, of one Father, redeemed by the same blood, journeying to the same happy land, there to sit down at the same table with the Lord, to mingle among the same holy company of the redeemed in heaven, and, in one sweet and hallowed fellowship, to sing the praises of God and the Lamb for ever and ever." And while she thus breathed this warm and affectionate spirit to all whose hearts had been changed by a simple belief of the truth as it is in Jesus, to whatever denomination of Christians they might belong, her love at the same time to the world, to those who were perishing for lack of knowledge, to those who had never experienced that peace and joy which is bestowed only through a believing look to Calvary, and who were exposing their precious never-dying souls to eternal ruin and misery every moment, by rejecting the salvation fully and freely offered to them in the gospel, was no less striking. Frequently, in the dusk of evening, she would lay aside her needle or her book, and proceed to the parlor window, from which she could obtain a view of the more crowded parts of the city, and after remaining there for some time, contemplating in silence the interesting picture of human life which stretched out on either side of her, on the vast multitude of immortal beings hurrying to and fro on the bustling stage of life, pursuing the affairs and commerce of the world, she would ask such questions as the following: "How many of these precious and deathless souls shall have passed into eternity before the expiration of another week; and who shall be first? How many in the course of another twelvemonth; and who shall they be? And of that vast multitude, how many in thirty years shall be in the land of the living? And to what place are they hurrying? Are they crowding to endless life, or endless death; to eternal happiness, or eternal woe?"

Growing daily in grace and in the knowledge of the Lord, Mrs. Little's love for perishing souls and her desire for their salvation exhibited themselves correspondingly through the medium of increasing active operations on her part. The cultivation of principles of method and order in the performance of all her actions, whether these were trifling or otherwise, being a propensity to which her mind was constitutionally much addicted, she was in the habit of using a memorandum-book, for the purpose of marking down all her weekly household expenses; and she made it a rule with herself, that whenever these expenses were less than a given sum per week, she would appropriate the difference—in addition to the usual weekly sum which she devoted to religious purposes—to the spread of the truth as it is in Jesus. The result of this resolution was, that I soon observed her denying herself many of her usual comforts, and would remark to her in a jocular manner, that she was becoming very penurious. "Ah," she would reply, turning the joke aside, "ah, who can estimate the value of even one immortal soul; what is it not worth? If God gave his Son, and Jesus gave himself to die, for the salvation of souls, is it too much for those for whom he died to deny their poor perishing bodies a few of these passing comforts for the same blessed purpose?" Any intelligence, consequently, of the progress of Christ's kingdom, either at home or abroad, afforded her peculiar delight. She watched especially, with deep interest, the growing disposition on the part of many Scottish Christians, for a more practical exhibition to perishing sinners of the saving truth as it is in Jesus; being convinced that the great object for which the church on earth exists is to preach the gospel, to make known the "good news" to the unconverted throughout the world. The intelligence of a sinner having found peace by a view of the simple truth as it is in Jesus, conveyed to her mind an amount of enjoyment that the mere things of this world cannot bestow. The letters we received from time to time from brother Simon, at Selkirk, regarding the work of conversion in the south of Scotland, were quite a feast to her soul. An esteemed friend, Mr. William Bathgate, who sometimes happened to be present when these letters were received, informed me, shortly after the death of Mrs. Little, that when those portions of them were read which immediately alluded to some anxious inquirer having found peace in the all-atoning blood of the Lamb, he would observe her eye kindle and sparkle with delight. Regarding the work of the Lord here alluded to, Mrs. Little thus writes in a letter to her aunt, Mrs. Cumming, dated November 12, 1841: "I am happy to hear you have had such nice meetings, and that Mr. Wilson of Denholm was staying with you, and that you have been much refreshed. I hear that Mr. M'Dougal, from Edinburgh, is at present among you; is he doing much good? When you write, let me know about these matters, *and if there are many conversions.*"

With regard to the pleasures and amusements of the world, it is needless to say that these did not in her estimation possess any features of attraction: on the contrary, she considered all such sources of enjoyment as only vain and momentary resorts of the unhappy and restless soul in a state of estrangement from God; and to the Christian, as trifles quite unworthy the attention of an immortal being, destined to occupy throughout all eternity such a noble and dignified position with angels and archangels in the courts of heaven; and yet a greater amount of cheerfulness and of solid happiness could scarcely be found in the possession of one mind, than reigned in her bosom. Looking continually through the cross of Christ to a "well-pleased" God, she daily and hourly enjoyed the refreshings of the waters of salvation on her soul; conscious, however, of the evil tendencies of her own heart to pursue the fleeting and perishing vanities of time, and to draw her mind away from the great realities of eternity; and conscious also, that she was unable, for a single moment, to stand in her own strength, she devoted a considerable time daily to secret prayer. Jesus on Calvary, taking away the sin of the world, was the last object that left her mental vision at night, and the first that met the eye of her soul in the morning. Every forenoon, also, she was in the habit of unobservedly withdrawing herself for a considerable time to her closet, to hold secret communion with the God and Saviour of her soul, to confess her sins to Him who was faithful to forgive them, and to ask the guidance and direction of the Holy Spirit in all her affairs; and thus, living closely to God, placing all her confidence in him as in a father, filled with his Spirit, and, through Jesus, looking forward to the glorious hope set before her in the gospel, did she enjoy that cheerfulness of heart, that calm and peace of mind already referred to, which nothing of a worldly nature ever seemed able in the least degree to disturb, and which, joined to a naturally amiable disposition, threw a soft and hallowed sweetness into all her actions, and at once—though unconsciously to herself—endeared her to all around.

Mrs. Little's own experience thus testified that the peace and joy of the gospel, the calm of a pardoned soul through the merits of Jesus, were far beyond the world's purchase, and that, whatever might be one's riches and earthly possessions, he was after all but a poor, poor man, and in the prospect of death a wretched and miserable man, to whose bosom the "glad tidings of great joy" had never been admitted: and in alluding to the various methods vainly resorted to by the world for the purpose of producing happiness, and of filling up that vacuum in the mind which nothing but the gospel of Jesus can fill, that craving of the soul after happiness which nothing but the waters of salvation can satisfy, she would kindly and affectionately remark, "Oh, if they just knew that 'without money and without price' they might obtain happiness to their souls, and that, too, in the most plentiful abundance and of the richest and most exalted kind, if they would but accept of it at the hands of Jesus, in whom alone it is to be found!"

The following hymn, expressive of her views and feelings in this respect, being at all times a favorite in her estimation, scarcely an evening was allowed to pass in which she did not sing, in her own sweet and melodious way, the verses which follow in connection with the delightful and pathetic Scotch air, entitled "Auld Lang Syne;" thus blending with the finest music the sweetest specimens of sacred poetry.

"Ho, ye that thirst, approach the spring
Where living waters flow—
Free to that sacred fountain all
Without a price may go,

Without a price may go,
Without a price may go;
Free to the sacred fountain all
Without a price may go.

"How long to streams of false delight
Will ye in crowds repair?
How long your strength and substance waste
On trifles light as air?
On trifles light as air, etc.

"My stores afford those rich supplies
That health and pleasure give;
Incline your ear and come to me,
The soul that hears shall live,
The soul that hears shall live, etc.

* * * * * * * *

"Seek ye the Lord while yet his ear
Is open to your call;
While offered mercy still is near,
Before his footstool fall,
Before his footstool fall, etc.

She experienced much enjoyment from the application of various favorite pieces of Scottish music to a number of hymns which appear in Dr. Wardlaw's collection, but especially of the foregoing she was passionately fond; and even in the dead hour of the night, when the din of the busy city had died away amid the silence of midnight, did Jesus become the subject of her contemplations. She would talk about Him who had nowhere to lay his head, and sing a verse of this her favorite "Song of Zion" in her sweetest and softest strain, before again committing herself to sleep, and to the care and protection of Him whose eye "neither slumbers nor sleeps." Frequently have I heard the silence of midnight broken in this way; and afterwards, on her death-bed, when physical strength would permit, she would employ short intervals of relief in singing the same verses in connection with the music already referred to.

To this peculiar habit which Mrs. Little cherished, of connecting sacred poetry with what is called "profane" music, not a few excellent Christians may be found to object. The practice was simply the result of a conscientious conviction on her part, that music in itself was, properly speaking, neither sacred nor profane, and that its recognition under one or the other of these denominations depended entirely on the character of the words or poetry with which it was associated; and also the conviction that our finest national music might be made subservient to the promotion of God's glory, and to the spiritual and social enjoyment of his people. It was strictly on this principle that she indulged in the habit alluded to.

Making the Bible her daily study, Mrs. Little possessed a clear and extensive acquaintance with the word of God; and when there was occasion for a reference to any particular passage of Scripture, she would quietly turn to the chapter and verse required, without the least appearance of difficulty; and with regard to the grand truth of the Bible, the way of salvation through the atonement of Jesus Christ, her clear and simple views of it enabled her to be useful in directing inquirers to "the Lamb of God, who taketh away the sin of the world."

A short while previous to her being laid on her death-bed, she took a deep interest in the eternal welfare of an individual, for whom she had the highest esteem and respect, but with the ground of whose hopes for eternity she was by no means satisfied; on the contrary, she was convinced that, although a member of a Christian church, she had yet to know what it was to be "born again," and to rejoice in the liberty of the gospel. The individual referred to, however, being considerably more than three times the age of Mrs. Little; the latter, fearing apparently that her youth might act unfavorably on the judgment of her aged friend in any attempt to deal faithfully with her, and to direct her attention to the state of her soul before God, made an arrangement with a Christian brother of greater experience, and more advanced in years, to enter on the duty and privilege of bringing the gospel to bear upon her soul; while she, Mrs. Little, would, in her closet, supplicate God to direct the conversation by his Holy Spirit, and make it result in the conversion to Jesus of the soul about whose eternal welfare she had manifested such a deep interest. This was done, and her prayers were answered: in the course of a day or two, the individual referred to, who had been a member of a Christian church for upwards of forty years, but who confessed she had never before known the joyful sound, became a new creature in Christ Jesus.

CHAPTER IV.

COMMENCEMENT OF HER ILLNESS—RESIGNATION—PARTING WITH HER CHILD—INCREASING HAPPINESS—THE ILLNESS AND DEATH OF HER CHILD—CHEERFULNESS UNDER THE TRIAL—PROSPECT OF PARTING WITH HER HUSBAND—MESSAGE TO HER FRIENDS—INTENSE PHYSICAL SUFFERING—PEACE OF MIND—CONSCIOUSNESS OF HER SAFETY IN JESUS.

Such is a brief outline of Mrs. Little's experience, from a short period before the time when the first ray of divine truth dawned upon her mind at Selkirk, on the occasion formerly alluded to, down to the latter end of 1841. She is now to be viewed under totally different circumstances—circumstances, alas, of the most sad and melancholy nature. On the evening of the Sabbath, the nineteenth of December, 1841, she became a joyful mother; and to all appearance was under the progress of recovery, till the following Tuesday, when she was seized with an inflammatory disease, generally known by the name of "puerperal fever." To the mind of her judicious medical attendant, the symptoms of the disease were decidedly of an unfavorable character, which naturally created anxiety on the part of her friends. With a view, therefore, of making provision against the threatened approach of danger, so far as the employment of human means was concerned, it was thought advisable both by Dr. Maxwell and myself, that advantage should be taken of additional medical advice. The assistance of Dr. King, another medical gentleman of great respectability and talent, and possessing a high character in his profession, was consequently immediately procured, and both of these gentlemen attended her, down to the period of her death, with an attention and an interest which the surviving friends of Mrs. Little cannot remember but with feelings of lively gratitude. Dr. King's first view of the case coinciding with the matured opinion previously expressed by Dr. Maxwell, was not calculated to mitigate the anxiety thus created. Notwithstanding, however, the appearance of these unfavorable symptoms, the youth of Mrs. Little, and the formerly healthy character of her constitution, presented to the minds of her medical attendants grounds upon which they thought they were entitled to build considerably strong hopes of ultimate recovery. On my expressing these hopes to her, she replied, "I rather think I am seriously ill, and I cannot say whether I shall ever get better; but I am in good hands, and whatever is the will of the Lord, let him do it: I am quite willing either to live or die, whatever is his will; he doeth all things well; blessed be his holy name." On another occasion, with the view of ascertaining the state of her own mind regarding her prospects of recovery, I inquired if she herself entertained hopes of her own restoration to health, or if she was anticipating consequences of an unfavorable character. "Well," said she, in her usual composed and deliberate manner, "well, I am not quite sure, scarcely ever having had any illness of any kind before; I really do not know, with any thing like certainty, whether I am dangerously ill or not; perhaps I am not so very ill, after all. But this at least I know, that I am perfectly willing either to live or to die, whatever is the Lord's will."

In the course of a few days, our anxiety was considerably deepened: her mind began to wander; and the symptoms of the fever manifested, in every respect, a more alarming appearance. Under this distressing state of mind she continued to labor, more or less, for nearly the space of a week; after which she again recovered entire possession of the use of all her faculties, and they never after, for a single moment, forsook her. In other respects, however, the alarming symptoms in no degree abated; on the contrary she became more and more fevered; her pulse was still moving upwards, and her sufferings were more severe. Under these circumstances, as was to be expected, I was deeply distressed about her, and being but seldom absent from her bedside, enjoyed many opportunities of conversing with her on subjects of the highest importance to a human being. Her conversation on these occasions was always of the most cheering and refreshing character; and whenever the name of Jesus was mentioned, a sweet and grateful smile would gently pass over her countenance; and frequently, when talking about the love of Christ, about his leaving heaven, and for upwards of thirty years dwelling in the likeness of and among men, suffering meekly their reproaches and at last dying for their sins, she would, notwithstanding her severe sufferings, become so animated and happy, that, to all appearance, the fact of her lying helpless on a bed of affliction, for the time entirely disappeared from her mind.

Expectations had been entertained by her medical attendants that the expiration of about three weeks from the commencement of the fever would, in all probability, bring with it a change, either confirming our fears or strengthening our hopes of her ultimate recovery. To that period, which was now approaching, we looked forward with the deepest solicitude. To any such feeling of anxiety the mind of Mrs. Little, however, was an entire stranger; confidently believing that God, who had given such amazing proofs of his infinite love to a guilty world, would not afflict any of his children, unless that affliction was intended to be productive of ultimate benefit to the subject of it, she lay entirely passive under his rod, patiently and meekly awaiting his divine pleasure, either to restore her to health, or to make her pass through the "dark valley of the shadow of death;" and although, with her knowledge, I was in the habit of daily retiring into another room with the doctors, for the purpose of receiving the report regarding their patient, she was almost never heard to make the least inquiry of me, on my return to her bedroom, whether their statements were of a favorable or of an adverse character. Our hopes were now doomed to disappointment; the time referred to arrived, and she was evidently getting worse; her pulse was in no way abated, but rather more rapid than otherwise, and her physical sufferings were more intense than they had been hitherto.

Up to this time, the child, at the recommendation of the doctors, had been occasionally nursed by Mrs. Little; it was now deemed expedient to remove the babe altogether to the house of the nurse; and it was on this occasion that the existence in Mrs. Little's own mind, of convictions that her case was of a hopeless character, were for the first time indicated. Just as the nurse was about to leave with the child, Mrs. Little requested her to bring it to her bedside; which being done, she fondly embraced her unconscious infant, kissed it, and on handing it back to the nurse, said, "Good by, my dear Jane; I shall never see you again." Mrs. Little had now been upwards of three weeks in a most distressed condition, and every day was apparently adding to her severe sufferings. Her mind, however, was still enjoying the most perfect tranquillity; in proportion as the sufferings of her body increased, her soul appeared to rise in the scale of happiness, and to a loftier and purer state of sanctification and enjoyment; and she would allude to her approaching dissolution with the utmost composure. One day she was referring to that solemn crisis in her history as being in her own opinion not far distant, when the servant-girl happened to come into the bedroom on some errand. On observing the young woman, Mrs. Little abruptly broke off the conversation, and requesting her to come near her bedside, she gave her all her ordinary directions, in her usually exact and orderly way, entering with the utmost minuteness into every little particular, just as if nothing whatever was the matter. On the girl leaving the room, she immediately resumed the conversation regarding her own death, as if no interruption had taken place, with the most perfect cheerfulness, and with as much coolness and composure as when talking to the girl a few minutes before about the most ordinary domestic affairs.

After a few days more of bodily suffering,

but spiritual enjoyment on the part of Mrs. Little, it pleased the Lord to visit us with another severe and unlooked-for affliction, which might have been expected to disturb in some measure that extraordinarily peaceful and happy state of mind which she had hitherto possessed. Information having been received from the nurse that the child was taken suddenly ill, and with every appearance of danger, another medical gentleman, residing in the locality, was immediately called upon to attend the young sufferer, and his report of the child was of such a character as to leave us but slender encouragement to indulge hopes of her recovery. The doctor also, having learned from the nurse the very precarious circumstances in which Mrs. Little was placed, was of opinion that to keep her ignorant of the dangerous state of her child would, under the circumstances, be advisable ; lest the communication of the painful intelligence might be productive of agitation, and otherwise be attended with undesirable results. Calculating, however, on her resignation to the will of God hitherto, and fearing that, if our worst apprehensions regarding the child were confirmed, the shock which the intelligence of its death would give to her feelings might be more severe than if her mind were prepared by a previous knowledge of its illness, it was deemed more prudent to acquaint Mrs. Little with the real facts; and accordingly I did so, in a way as gentle as truth would admit of, when, in the most calm and submissive manner, she merely replied, "The Lord's will be done; let him do with her whatever to his wisdom seemeth fit."

Next day the little sufferer, after only twenty hours' illness, breathed her last. And now the painful duty devolved upon me to acquaint her with the mournful tidings; and Oh, how painful to a fond husband, to intimate to the dying and beloved wife of his bosom the death of their lovely and only child! Considering the strong attachment Mrs. Little had manifested for her child, I was deeply distressed in being obliged to give her the melancholy information. The performance of the painful duty, however, could not be avoided; and after a little delay I entered the room, and sitting down by her bedside, took her by the hand as usual and quietly acquainted her with the mournful news. Anticipating the effects which might naturally be expected to follow the communication of intelligence of such a nature, I was prepared to direct her mind to such an aspect of her bereavement as I believed was best calculated to reconcile her to this new and sudden affliction. From the performance of this task, however, I was happily relieved. The moment the information escaped from my lips, she looked up in my face, and with a sweet and heavenlike smile on her countenance, exclaimed, "Aye, aye, and has my dear Jane got to glory before me?" She then entered into a long and interesting conversation with me about the mysterious ways of God, and the infinite wisdom displayed in all his doings; spoke of her own afflictions only as manifestations of his love; and, in alluding to the death of her child, cheerfully acknowledged, that if we could be permitted to get a prospective view of the plans and purposes of Jehovah, this would just be the very time when we should not only not regret, but should even desire her removal from the world: perhaps God foresaw that a thousand trials and dangers would beset her path through life; that, when we least expected, death might snatch her away without a moment's notice; that she might, if spared to riper years, refuse the glorious offer in the gospel, and die an unbeliever; and consequently, her never-dying soul be consigned to that awful pit of misery and despair, where a ray of hope never enters, where the worm dieth not, and where the flame of Jehovah's wrath burneth for ever and ever.

Now, what was the real state of the case? It was true she had lost the little darling of her heart, so far as time was concerned; but then her child had been relieved from all the sorrows, the trials, and temptations of a wicked world: and to what land had she gone? Let the Son of God himself reply: "Suffer little children to come unto me, and forbid them not, for of such is the kingdom of God;" a glorious and soul-cheering statement, calculated not only to cause the heart of the bereaved mother to leap for joy, and calm the heavings of her troubled bosom, but even to make her rejoice over the empty cradle of her darling child. And again, "All things work together for good to them that love God;" a declaration which to the believer is altogether precious, and a balm to every wound. During this conversation she was uncommonly cheerful and animated, and frequently exclaimed, "O, yes—O, yes, He doeth all things well; blessed be his holy name. I shall not, I cannot murmur for the loss of my dear child; it is God who has done it all, and he cannot err."

Two days after this the child was committed to the silence of the tomb, in the new cemetery at Sight-hill. During these two days Mrs. Little's conversation, when physical suffering would permit, manifested the same cheerfulness which had hitherto characterized it, and no one, unacquainted with the circumstances, could have discovered from her manner and countenance that she was the subject of such a trying bereavement. Jesus was the object of her joy and hope, and she felt that he would never leave her; and truly could she sing,

"In all my troubles sharp and strong,
My soul to Jesus flies;
My anchor-hold is firm in him
When swelling billows rise:
His comforts bear my spirits up,
I trust a faithful God;
The sure foundation of my hope
Is in my Saviour's blood."

On my return from the funeral of the child, she inquired particularly about the exact place where the body of her "dear Jane" was laid; anticipating, probably, that in a few days she would be called to lie by the side of her child. She knew the spot; we had walked together among the tombs, and talked about the dead, in the same place. On this, as on former occasions, she conversed in her usual happy manner; indeed, so cheerful was her resignation to the will of God, that she was never afterwards heard to allude to the death of her child. When her aunt, Mrs. Cumming, from Selkirk, arrived, she merely observed, "Oh, aunt, if you had only seen the sweet little creature!" And down to her death, ten days after, she never again alluded to the subject.

The very painful circumstances in which Mrs. Little was now placed were calculated to put to the strictest test her confidence in God: for five weeks she had been the subject of very severe sufferings; on every side the storm of affliction was still raging even more furiously than ever; her body was now feeble and emaciated, and she lay as helpless as an infant, almost unable to effect the slightest movement of any part of her frame. The earth had already closed over her lovely child, and every thing around was betokening that she herself would in a few days be lowered down to the same dark and lonely resting-place: her mind, nevertheless, was still unmoved; all within was calm and still, all peaceful and serene; and while afflictions were darkening on either side, and her body writhing with pain, her soul was resting with divine tranquillity on the finished work of her Saviour. On one occasion, when suffering under the most excruciating tortures, she smiled and exclaimed, "Well, well, it is all one; as my body sinks my soul riseth."

This progress in her mind to a more perfect and exalted state of happiness and holiness, had always been observable from the very commencement of her illness; it was now, however, more strikingly manifest. Every hour, as her body became more feeble and drew nearer to the grave, her soul became more and more like the divine image of her Saviour, and her joy and peace more like the joy and peace of heaven. To this delightful and heavenward progress of her mind, only one slight interruption occurred during her whole illness; and considering all the circumstances, this could scarcely be wondered at. Our union had been of the most happy and endearing character; it had existed little more than a twelvemonth, and we had looked forward with delightful anticipations to many years of sweet companionship with each other: all these were to be blasted, and we were now to be parted never again to meet in time. Such thoughts had been crossing her mind one day as I was sitting alone by her bedside, when, taking me by the hand with an affectionate grasp, and the tears rushing over her pale cheek, she exclaimed, in a tone of painful anguish, "Oh, my dear John, how shall I leave you? how shall we part? Oh, I cannot, I cannot, I cannot;" and, weeping and sobbing, she continued to exclaim, "Oh, I cannot, I cannot." I immediately endeavored, so far as I was able, to lead her mind to Him who alone could enable us to bear and to do all his will; and to show her, that since she had found such a sweet Saviour, such a faithful and loving friend as Jesus, no other was worth weeping for. On hearing the name of Jesus pronounced, she immediately became quite calm and composed; and having occasion, in the course of a few minutes, to go into another room, I overheard her in my absence singing, in a sweet and mellow tone, the following verse:

"I leave the world without a tear,
Save for the friends I hold most dear;
To heal their sorrows, Lord, descend,
And to the friendless prove a friend."

On my return to her bedroom she said, "Oh, I see I have just been looking away from Jesus; I know there is no variableness nor shadow of turning with him. Oh, yes, I have just been looking away from him, and I much fear we have too often done so; making idols of and loving each other more than Him who first loved us and gave himself for us: perhaps that is the reason why God is going to separate us so early; he will not permit his creatures to worship idols, and no doubt we have been doing so. Whatever he does, however, I know it will be the best for us in the end; let his will therefore be done." She had now resumed all her former equanimity, and entered into conversation with her usual cheerfulness; and whenever I cast my eye upon her, either in going in or coming out of the room, she would smile and give a gentle bow with her head, just as if she had been saluting a friend passing in the street and nothing whatever was the matter.

About seven o'clock on the Wednesday morning previous to her death, Mrs. Little being asleep, and being myself much fatigued, having remained up with her during the night, I intended to embrace the opportunity thus afforded to indulge in a little repose. I had only been in bed for a few minutes, when to my surprise, Mrs. Little began to sing in a strain the most beautiful and melodious I thought I had ever heard. Starting up and leaning on my arm, I looked towards her for a few minutes; her eyes were shut, and a gentle smile played on her countenance. I was unable, however, to distinguish the words whose heavenly sounds were flowing so sweetly from her lips. In a few minutes, and all in an instant, she paused, and burst out into ejaculations expressive sometimes of the most extraordinary wonder and amazement, at others of the most rapturous delight, and exclaiming, "Oh, what is yonder—what is yonder? what glory! it is not only the happiness, but the glory that is yonder! What a scene—what a place!" At length she seemed to be so overwhelmed with delight and amazement, that she was unable to articulate. It turned out that she had been dreaming, and that in her dream she thought she had obtained the privilege of a view of the celestial country. Just as she awoke, brother Robert happened to come in from the adjoining room, when she said to him, "Robert, I have just been in heaven, and Oh, what have I seen; what a blessed place! And whom do you think I saw? I saw my dear little Jane there. Oh, if you had just seen the sweet little darling, how happy she was:" thus showing that, whether awake or asleep, her thoughts were but little engaged with the concerns of the world. Next day brother Robert being obliged to leave for Selkirk, asked, on taking leave of her, if she wished to send any communication to her friends there. In a solemn and emphatic tone of voice, she replied, "Yes, I have *one* message to send to them, and *only one*, and it is this: just tell them all to believe in the Lord Jesus Christ, and they shall be saved." In the course of the evening she became to all appearance considerably worse, and expressed her conviction that death was now near at hand. After a night of severe suffering, she enjoyed a little repose in the morning, but no change for the better made its appearance; on the contrary, she was evidently fast sinking: of this fact no one appeared to be more convinced than herself. In the course of the following day, she lifted up her hand before her face, and, as a proof how near she was to glory, asked me to observe how very small and slender it was become. She also requested me to take from her finger her marriage-ring, as, in consequence of her hands being so much wasted, it would no longer remain in its place. As I reluctantly proceeded to comply with her painful request, the happy event which had placed the ring on her finger only a short twelvemonth before, and the melancholy circumstances under which it was now to be for ever removed, were subjects over which her mind appeared for the time to be musing; and as I silently stood by her bedside, wrapping in a piece of paper the now unheeded token of a past event, a tinge of melancholy slightly veiled her countenance, and the deep contemplative cast of her eye betrayed that mournful emotions were flitting across her soul. She said nothing, however, and after engaging in prayer she fell into a slight repose. Towards the evening, and on Saturday, the following day, her sufferings were very intense, more so indeed than they had ever yet been; and, with the exception of her head and one of her hands, she was unable to move any part of her body: her soul however was rising higher and higher in the scale of happiness; and on conversing with her I found her in possession of a peace and joy of mind beyond any thing I had ever before witnessed. On one occasion, when the sufferings of her body were more than usually severe and heart-rending, I was so much struck with the dignified serenity of her mind, that I was led to inquire why, under such severe bodily distress, she was experiencing what I thought was even more than her usual joy; looking up in my face, with an air of surprise at such a question, she replied emphatically, and in a joyful tone of voice, "John, I *know* in whom I have believed."

CHAPTER V.

PRAYER—ADVANTAGES DERIVED FROM IT—INCREASING PHYSICAL SUFFERINGS—THEIR ABATEMENT—STATE OF HER MIND—JESUS THE SOURCE OF HER JOY—APPARENT APPROACH OF DEATH—HER CONSCIOUSNESS OF IT—GOD'S PROMISES FULFILLED—THE LOVE OF CHRIST AND HER OWN INGRATITUDE—MESSAGE TO HER MEDICAL ATTENDANTS—THE TEXT FOR HER FUNERAL SERMON—PRAYER ANSWERED—THE WORK OF CHRIST.

Ever since, by the grace of God, Mrs. Little knew the truth as it is in Jesus, prayer was the most delightful exercise in which she engaged; from the period of her conversion down to the last moments of her life, her faith in the finished atonement of Jesus had never been alloyed by the presence of doubt in her mind: a cloud had never dimmed that clear and simple view of the work of Christ which first brought peace to her soul, and the consequent calm and joy which she experienced had never been disturbed. To her habits of frequent communion with God, and to her childlike confidence in all his promises, may be attributed in a great measure that delightful and cheerful state of mind which she possessed. With her eye constantly turned to "the Lamb of God, who taketh away the sin of the world," her soul revolved as it were continually round and round the cross of Calvary; and the more she beheld the sinless victim bleeding and dying there, "not only" for her sins—and for your sins, reader—but also "for the sins of the whole world," the more did she delight to come into the presence of that Almighty Being; because, through the sacrifice of his Son and equal, she saw divine justice completely satisfied for all her sins; through Calvary she could see a "well-pleased" God—through Calvary she could behold a smiling Father, a God of love, willing to protect her, rejoicing to watch over her, and waiting to receive her at last to himself. When Mr. Pullar, her esteemed pastor, or any of her brothers or sisters in the church, called at the house to make inquiries regarding her, she generally requested that the few minutes she was able to see them should be solely occupied in prayer; and during some of the last nights of her existence, I have known her to be at the throne of grace eight or ten times in as many hours. After every short interval of sleep, for some nights preceding her death, "Let us engage in prayer," were generally the first words which fell from her lips. In alluding to this exercise a day or two before she expired, she said, "It brings me always so near to God, and I feel just so very close to Jesus, I don't know how it is, and so happy, that I really cannot describe it." A considerable portion of her time appeared to be also occupied in silent meditation: her aunt, Mrs. Cumming, would sometimes, when sitting in the room alone with her, observe her shut her eyes for a few moments, then open them and with a sweet serenity and holy joy on her countenance calmly and steadily look towards heaven for perhaps the space of a minute, and then again shut and open them alternately for a few times in the same way, while her thoughts appeared to be engaged in sweet communion with the God and Saviour of her soul. While thus in attendance with her one night, her aunt inquired if there was any portion of Scripture which she would wish to be read. "Yes," she replied, "you may read the first chapter of John's gospel: it is there I think where so much is said of Christ; and the words, 'Behold the Lamb of God who taketh away the sin of the world,' are repeated." She requested her aunt to read also the first chapter of the epistle to the Hebrews; saying, "In that chapter you will see how much glory is given to the Son."

For forty wearisome days and nights she had now lain prostrate on a bed of affliction, under the severity of which it surprised even the doctors themselves that her earthly existence had been prolonged for such a length of time; and during all that long period a murmur was never heard to escape her lips. She frequently, however, gave expression to the extreme agony to which the daily shifting of her position subjected her; this cannot be wondered at, when it is considered that latterly a single touch of the finger on many parts of her body produced pain. One day, after the doctors had been changing her position, which they desired frequently to be done, I observed her weeping; and on making inquiry for the cause of her tears, she replied that she feared she was not patient enough under the hands of the doctors: the agony, she said, was very, very great; but to complain was unlike her divine Master. On Saturday evening she became very restless; a deep hectic flush rested on her cheek; her respiration was fast and difficult; the copious streams of perspiration oozing from her fevered forehead required the constant application of the sponge; and altogether she presented a heart-rending spectacle of suffering. And, what rendered the picture even more painful, she exclaimed two or three times in a tone of agony, "Oh, could you not lift me up? Could you not lift me up? Oh, do lift me up—do lift me up!"

In this distressing condition Mrs. Little continued till nearly eleven o'clock, when she became less restless, and the fever began apparently to subside. She now requested that the doctor's orders to alter the position of her body, which were formerly attended to about the same hour in the evening, might be dispensed with, and that she might be permitted to lie as she was now doing on her back, till death should put an end to her sufferings; "for," said she, "the sorting is so painful, and besides it can do me no good, for I know I shall soon be away." We now saw that all human effort to mitigate her sufferings or prolong her life was unavailing, and that we could do nothing more than wipe the perspiration from her forehead and passively await the closing of her eye by the hand of death. By this time the intense bodily suffering under which she had been previously laboring was very considerably abated, and, much exhausted, she sunk into a state of light repose, in which she continued till about one in the morning. When she awoke at that time, she appeared to be considerably refreshed, and to my great joy and contrary to expectation asked for a small piece of biscuit and a little wine, which she received and appeared to relish. On our presenting her with the biscuit and wine, she said, "Oh, how very easy I feel to-day; I am as comfortable this morning as I was restless last night: and then how happy; Oh, I really cannot describe it!" And on talking about Jesus, her usual theme, such a sense of the love of God in having condescended, "without money and without price," to provide a Saviour for her, unworthy as she felt herself to be—such a sense of the sufficiency of Christ's death to wash all her sins away, of God as completely satisfied with that death for all her transgressions, of entire confidence and safety for her soul in the finished work of the cross, appeared to occupy her mind—that, in the words of the Psalmist, literally her "mouth was filled with laughter;" for as she spoke of "the Lamb of God who taketh away the sins of the world," she could not desist from smiling under the feeling of joy and gratitude which she experienced. Mrs. Little now became so cheerful, and conversed in such a firm and healthy tone of voice, while pain and sickness to a great extent appeared to have left her, that a hope even yet arose in my mind that a change for the better had actually taken place; and under this impression I went to Mrs. Cumming, who was sleeping in the adjoining room, and informed her of the favorable symptoms which had made their appearance. Shortly after, Mrs. Cumming rose, quite delighted with the information which had just been conveyed to her, and I now intended taking a short repose, which Mrs. Cumming's presence and the apparently favorable turn of circumstances now offered; but I had just lain down with revived hopes, and begun to picture in my mind her who was so near and dear to me again restored to her wonted health, when Mrs. Cumming approached my bedside and informed me that she feared I had been mistaken, and that immediate danger was to all appearance approaching. Startled at such painful intelligence, I rose hurriedly, unwilling to part with my former hopes; but, alas, Mrs. Cumming's apprehensions turned out to be too true: the favorable change had only been in appearance—had only been the hushing of the storm after the wreck was completed. The abatement two hours before of the severe suffering above mentioned, it appeared had been the commencement of mortification, and the still rapid decrease of that suffering only served to mark its onward progress, and to inform us that death was closely following in the rear; and the now icy hand, the pale lip, and the cold sweat that bedewed her calm and youthful countenance, but too truly echoed the sad and melancholy tale.

It was now two o'clock, and never did such a morning dawn upon her existence; never before did she awake to the possession of a joy so deep, so pure, so heavenly; her wanderings through the wilderness of sin and suffering were now closing behind her, and not far hence she could descry with the eye of faith the promised land, the heavenly country; she could see, through the vista of a few short hours, the turrets of the golden, the eternal city, to which the finished work of Emmanuel was bearing her in triumph away. As the sound of "past three" was heard from the city watchmen away in the distance, Canaan's land was nearer and brighter in her view, and the joyful shout of the jubilee trumpet swelling more loudly upon her ear. Onward as the morning advanced, she still appeared to be rising into a higher and happier state of being. From one o'clock, the time at which she awoke, up to eight o'clock in the morning, she was frequently engaged in prayer; at times she would converse with us in her usual happy manner about the delightful theme, Jesus Christ and him crucified, every succeeding conversation developing more and more the peace which passeth all understanding, the joy of dying in the Lord, which her mind possessed. The sun rose about eight o'clock, and every thing indicated that, before he descended in the west, the sun of Mrs. Little's earthly career would be set for ever, and her soul disembodied and in the world of spirits. Of this Mrs. Little appeared also to have not the smallest doubt: the doctors' medicines were now set aside, as being of no more use; the wine and biscuit, which had been her only nourishment for some days previous, were also laid away; she could drink no more wine until she would drink it new in her Father's kingdom. She felt as if she had nothing more to do with her mortal body, or with any thing in this world; and all that now remained for us to do was to wipe away the cold perspiration that oozed from her forehead, to converse with her when she desired, to engage in prayer with her at intervals, as she requested, and to wait till she could say,

"The hour of my departure's come,
I hear the voice that calls me home."

In these circumstances, the doctors, on making their morning call about nine o'clock, found us, when they merely informed us that their attendance, they were sorry to say, was now no more necessary, and that we must make up our minds for the worst ere very long.

The day was now evidently arrived when the truth of that religion which was her joy in health, her support in affliction, her happiness in time, and her hope for eternity, was to receive another glorious confirmation; when the blessed promises of the Almighty to his people, "I will never leave thee nor forsake thee;" "when thou passest through the waters, I will be with thee;" "the sting of death shall be taken away;" "fear thou not, for I am with thee; be not dismayed, for I am thy God," were to be fulfilled to the very letter. Death, the last enemy, was now gradually but steadily moving forward to take possession of his victim: calmly and unmovedly she viewed its approach; she already felt its cold touch, but she heeded it not. Considering it merely as the separation of her soul and body, its sting was entirely taken away, and instead of waiting its arrival with fear and terror, she did so with joy and pleasure—instead of anticipating it as the most appalling and critical hour in her history, she contemplated it as the happiest moment in her worldly existence; she looked upon death only as the messenger that was to announce to her friends who were left behind, her entrance into the land of eternal felicity—as the signal that was to open for her admittance the gates of the new Jerusalem, and to usher her into the company of God and of the Lamb, of angels and archangels, and of the mighty host of the redeemed who sing around the throne for ever and ever—as the voice that was to proclaim, "All things are ready;" "Come, ye blessed of my Father, inherit the kingdom prepared for you from the foundation of the world;" "enter ye into the joy of your Lord."

Every vestige of bodily suffering having now disappeared, and lying, as she had done for some time, on a hydrostatic or floating bed, she expressed herself with the utmost thankfulness and gratitude, that she was suffering no pain whatever, and that she was enjoying as much bodily ease and comfort as it was possible for any person to do, even in the possession of the most perfect health. This entire freedom from physical suffering might be accounted for by the extent to which mortification had now advanced; her whole body, with the exception of her head and chest and one arm, was now become cold as lead—lifeless and almost insensible to the touch. Her body, her affliction, and her approaching dissolution, did not now appear to occupy any portion of her attention: her whole theme was again about the Saviour; she spoke as if it baffled her utmost stretch of conception to comprehend the depth of that love which induced the Son of God to leave his throne in the heavens, to hide his glory in human form, to be born in a manger, to be despised and reviled, and even to die as a degraded criminal on Calvary, for the very beings who had violated his laws, rebelled against him, and were his enemies in every form. The more she beheld the Saviour in his true character, the more base, the more ungrateful, the more sinful and unworthy she saw herself to be. On contemplating that marvellous love, and comparing it with her own ingratitude, with how little she had done for the cause of Christ compared with what she might have done; and on considering how few perishing souls she had entreated to stop and listen to the "good news," that they might believe them, and live and die rejoicing, and go to glory as she was now doing, she would look upon herself as the chief of sinners, as a poor worthless being; and, amazed that God could deign to love such a rebel, she would exclaim, "Wretch that I am!"

On another occasion she observed Mrs. Campbell, a lady of her acquaintance who had taken a deep interest in her, and had been most kind and unremitting in her attention to her during the whole period of her illness, to be in tears; when she said, "Weep not for me, Mrs. Campbell, I am not worth weeping for." She now mentioned the names of many of her friends, and alluded to their spiritual welfare with the most affectionate solicitude. At this time her whole mind appeared to be engrossed about the welfare of souls, whoever and wherever they were, and to manifest a deep and yearning anxiety to tell them about that Saviour, to accept of whom, as a *gift*, was life eternal—that Saviour who was willing and able to save them, and who had come for that very purpose; who had spilt that blood which "cleanseth from all sin," for their transgressions; and who was still following them with deep compassion, proclaiming through his word in accents of tenderest affection, to every sinner—and to you, unconverted reader—"God so loved the world, that he gave his only begotten Son, that *whosoever* believeth in him should not perish, but have everlasting life:" "Incline your ear and come unto me; hear, and your soul shall live:" "As I live, saith the Lord, I have no pleasure in the death of the wicked:" "Turn ye, turn ye; for why will ye die?"

Mrs. Little had had no opportunities of knowing any thing about the doctors, farther than the great kindness, care, and attention, with which they had treated her during her long illness; but, said she, "Tell Dr. Maxwell and Dr. King that I have felt very grateful for their kindness and unwearied attention to me during my illness; and tell them, from me, to believe in the Lord Jesus Christ and they shall be saved." This was the message which she had already sent to her friends in the south of Scotland, because it was the message which God had proclaimed to the whole world; and they were words which, from first to last, conveyed peace and joy to her own soul; and it was her burning and impatient desire, in her dying moments, to post the gladsome sound through every channel within her reach, to perishing souls, to one and all of the unconverted of the human family, if she had had it in her power, to the guiltiest sinner in existence, to the young and old, to the rich and poor, to the prince and the beggar, as the words were addressed to all. Shortly after she had requested me to convey this message to the doctors, she added, "But, of course, it is after I am dead when I wish you to deliver this message to the doctors: I shall be dead in a very little, and as soon as I am away you will do so, if they should happen then to come in, or on the first opportunity which may afterwards present itself." I said that I would do as she requested, when she sweetly remarked, "Very well," at the same time making a gentle bow of approbation with her head.

It may be here mentioned, in passing, that the latter amiable and highly respected gentleman here alluded to, little more than six months after he received this interesting communication from his young and dying patient, with which he was deeply affected, was himself summoned to the eternal world. He died in the following August, in the prime of life; and although his death was sudden and somewhat unexpected, he met its approach with great composure and resignation. A short while before he expired he placed his finger on his own pulse, and coolly informed his friends, by whom he was surrounded, when it ceased to beat. He was the brother of Dr. King, of Greyfriars' church, Glasgow; and was not only universally esteemed and respected by all who knew him, but was endeared to all with whom his official capacity brought him into contact.

Mrs. Little now mentioned that the Bible contained so many rich texts, that she felt some little difficulty in deciding which would prove most suitable and useful as a subject for her funeral-sermon. At length she thought that if Mr. Pullar should, for the benefit of the unconverted, improve the circumstance of her death on the following Sabbath, the words forming her message to her friends and the doctors, "Believe in the Lord Jesus Christ and thou shalt be saved," would probably be the most useful she could fix upon; and she accordingly decided that these words should form the text of her funeral-sermon. All this conversation took place with as much coolness and deliberation, on her part, as if she had been sitting as usual in her chair in the enjoyment of her wonted health, and talking about the most ordinary matters of every-day occurrence.

It was now eleven o'clock—it was the Sabbath—the church bells were chiming, and the people of God were wending their way to the house of prayer: circumstances which recalled to my mind the delight with which Mrs. Little was formerly accustomed to repair to the chapel on Sabbath morning, to meet and worship with her "dear brethren and sisters in Jesus," in the house of God. Many of her brethren and sisters in the church called at the door, inquiring with tears after their afflicted sister; while others waited in the street to receive the intelligence from those who called personally at the door; and the prayers of the assembled church were that day, as they had been frequently before, employed in her behalf. She was destined, however, never again to assemble with the church below: she was going to join for ever the church above; and, probably, while her brethren were that very day surrounding the table of the Lord on earth, and remembering "Jesus crucified," she would be sitting with the Saviour himself, at his own table in heaven, and gazing on "Jesus glorified." The kindness of her Christian friends with whom she was connected in church-fellowship, and who had manifested deep anxiety for her recovery, she appreciated much, although she felt herself unworthy of it.

A circumstance now occurred, which at first produced on the minds of those who were surrounding the death-bed of Mrs. Little, the greatest distress and alarm; but which was afterwards made the instrument of leading us to feel more and more our total dependence on God for every blessing; and of impressing us more deeply than ever with his wonderful character, and with the value and privilege of prayer. The following are the facts of the case, as nearly as the writer can remember: Mrs. Little's tongue began somewhat suddenly to swell, and in a short time the swelling had increased to such an extent that she was almost unable to articulate. The doctors, having considered their attendance no longer necessary, were not within our reach: we ourselves could do nothing to allay the swelling. To all appearance it was still increasing, and we were in the utmost dread, lest we should be called upon to suffer the terrible pain of seeing her literally choked, without being able to render her any assistance in averting such a calamity. In these circumstances we were led to apply to the heavenly Physician; we all united in earnestly supplicating God to remove the cause of our alarm, and to permit his handmaid to die under the absence of physical suffering. Our request was graciously granted; the swelling began to subside, and in a short time her tongue was reduced to its ordinary dimensions. The latter part of our petition, it will be afterwards observed, was also literally complied with, by the prayer-hearing and prayer-answering Jehovah.

Thus relieved, and with deep gratitude, she could now hear and talk of nothing but Jesus Christ and him crucified, through whom all blessings flow: he was all her delight and all her desire, and her whole soul appeared to be filled with the light of his countenance, and the presence of his Holy Spirit: "The Lamb of God, who taketh away the sins of the world," stood before her mind's eye in all his glory; he was the great sun and centre of the system of salvation, raised up in the view of a lost and fallen world, to whom, as the serpent-bitten Israelites looked to the brazen serpent and were healed, every sin-bitten soul is called upon to look and be saved. Any expressions falling from any of us, which seemed in the least degree to indicate that either the unconverted were looking for safety, or the believer for peace, to any other source than Jesus and him alone, she instantly detected. For example, she called her mother-in-law to her bedside, and said, "Mother, the young *may* die, but the old *must:* how do you feel now?" alluding to the peace of her soul with God through Jesus. Her mother-in-law, in replying to her interrogation, happened to make a remark to the effect that she had received much benefit from the many prayers she had heard presented to the throne of grace, on Mrs. Little's behalf, since the commencement of her illness. "From what?" the latter replied; "from what?" and appearing quite dissatisfied, gave us to understand that it was not from prayer, nor from any other work performed by us sinners, that peace and comfort flowed, but from *the work of Jesus alone*, which was *already finished* and completed, to the entire satisfaction of God's broken law; this was the "good news," the fountain of living water, and prayer was only the *instrument* by which that water was drawn up from the wells of salvation—

was only the channel through which nourishment was conveyed to the believer's soul: but prayer was not the nourishment itself; Jesus was the food and drink of the soul. These were not Mrs. Little's words, but convey the sentiments which her remarks expressed. It may perhaps be remembered that Mrs. Little, during the period she continued in an anxious and inquiring state of mind, had often placed the exercise of prayer in the room of Jesus, and was thereby led into a false and unscriptural position; which may account for the jealousy she always afterwards manifested, when the way of salvation was the subject of conversation, if any thing was mentioned indicating that the believer's hope rested on any thing more or less than the work of Christ alone. Sin coming wholly by man, and salvation wholly by Jesus Christ, were the two great separate truths which appeared ever to stand prominently before her mind; to her clear and simple views of which may be attributed much of that entire freedom from wavering and doubt, which, from the period when she first knew the truth, she had always enjoyed, and which now, in the face of death, appeared so prominently. In a short time, and at the close of another prayer, she said, "This is the Sabbath;" and remarking that there had been no allusion made to the Lord's day in the prayer which had just been concluded, requested that we should again engage in devotional exercise, and that the omission should be supplied. After this had been done, she again said, in a deep contemplative tone of voice, "This is the Sabbath." "Yes, my dear," replied her aunt, "you would hear that mentioned in the last prayer." "Yes, but that is not what I mean," Mrs. Little replied, in the same thoughtful manner; when Mrs. Cumming observed, that this was the day on which the Lord arose from the dead. "Yes, that's it, that's it," was Mrs. Little's response.

On another occasion, immediately after prayer had been presented to the throne of grace on her behalf, in which was employed a supplicatory expression, to the effect that if it was the Lord's pleasure now to remove her from the world, he would, *if consistent with his will*, take her to himself, she remarked with her usual candor and coolness of manner, to the individual who had led the devotion, that there was something decidedly wrong in his prayer. She mentioned that if she was about to die, and Jesus being the rock on which she was resting, there could be no *ifs* or doubts about God's willingness to take her to glory; and that it was impossible and contrary to his whole revealed character, to suppose that he could be unwilling to receive to himself each and all whose souls were reposing with perfect confidence on the atonement of his Son; and she knew in whom she was trusting. None of us having observed the expression referred to, we were rather surprised at such a quick discernment on her part of its erroneous and God-dishonoring character, and feelings of no ordinary solemnity and self-reproach were experienced by some of us, at least, from her unexpected remarks.

CHAPTER VI.

THE APPROACH OF DEATH—INTERVIEW WITH MRS. CAMPBELL—THE STATE OF HER MIND—SPIRITUAL JOY—PARTING REQUESTS—FORETASTE OF HEAVEN—HER DEATH—MEETING OF HER ACQUAINTANCES—HER FUNERAL—HER FUNERAL-SERMON—MANUSCRIPT WRITTEN BY MRS. LITTLE.

It was now half-past eleven o'clock, and the great and solemn crisis was evidently near at hand; her bosom heaved heavily, and the cold and clammy sweat bedewed her calm and peaceful countenance. For a few minutes she ceased to speak, the pale shadow of death was noiselessly stealing over her, and all was deep and solemn silence. Under the impression that the sound of her voice would never again fall on my ear, and that the painful separation which I had hitherto so much dreaded, was now about to take place, I involuntarily turned my face away from her, when her quick eye immediately observed me; and correctly apprehending the cause of my distress, she said in a sweet and gentle manner, "Do not be ill, my dear John, I am not going away just yet; do not be ill, do not be ill." As I turned again, and gazed on the face of her who had thus spoken, there was, in the very sweetness of her countenance, in the heavenliness of her eye, a something which seemed to forbid the heaving of a sigh or the shedding of a tear for her; something which seemed to say,

> "Let not your hearts with anxious thoughts
> Be troubled or dismayed."

"The Lord is my refuge and my fortress;" "the Lord is my light and my salvation;" and therefore, "though a host should encamp against me, my heart shall not fear." After the lapse of a minute or two, she requested Mrs. Campbell to come near to her bedside, and thus addressed her: "Mrs. Campbell, your great kindness and unwearied attention to me during my illness, I am unable to repay; but my wish and prayer is, that when you come to die, the Lord may bless you as he has blessed me on a dying bed; that you may then have that peace and joy which, by grace, I now possess; and that in heaven you may meet all your dear children who have gone before you." Mrs. Campbell, out of a family of ten beloved children, had already laid nine of them in the grave; and the tenth and last, a fine and intelligent boy three years of age, has also since been borne to the silent tomb. Mrs. Campbell, on taking this last farewell of her, was in tears; and on this coming under the observation of Mrs. Little, the latter said, "Weep not for me, Mrs. Campbell, for I am happy, happy, happy!" with a sweet expression of countenance, indicating in words,

"Take comfort, Christians, when your friends
In Jesus fall asleep;
Their better being never ends,
Why then dejected weep?
Why inconsolable, as those
To whom no hope is given?
Death is the messenger of peace,
And calls the soul to heaven."

She concluded her interview with this lady by making some affectionate inquiries regarding the spiritual welfare of Mr. Campbell, her husband.

Mrs. Little now presented a spectacle of the most intense interest; she spoke calmly and firmly, as usual, and every word which fell from her lips was laden with a dignity of meaning which the pen is unable correctly to describe. In alluding to the Saviour, and the glorious eternity which through his merits was awaiting her, the language she employed was so lofty and sublime, that I felt as if I were no longer in the presence of my earthly companion, or of a mere human being, but under the celestial voice of a glorified spirit, already within the portals of heaven and conversing in heaven's loftiest language, looking down on this our lower world with all its riches and honors as a vain and empty possession, and, compared with the glorious eternity that was now stretching out before her, as unworthy of a moment's notice, save for the myriads of deathless souls that were hurrying along its path on their way to endless life or endless misery; and while she thus discoursed in such sublime language, the profound and hallowed joy which filled her soul became deeper and deeper as death approached nearer and nearer. "Oh," she would exclaim, "Oh, I really cannot describe how happy I feel;" and when prayer was made at her bedside, she would turn up her eyes, beaming with deep and holy joy, towards heaven, and triumphantly wave her hand backward and forward before her face, while the calm and hallowed serenity of her countenance, and the steady gaze of her upturned eye, proclaimed that her thoughts were away in heaven, and that her soul was joyfully shouting, "O death, where is thy sting? O grave, where is thy victory?"

Up to this hour I had never been able to obtain from my mind a cordial and willing consent to give her up to God, or to say, with entire and unqualified sincerity, "Thy will be done;" but now, every shadow of reluctance was removed, and not only did I now feel perfectly reconciled to her, the nearest and dearest friend on earth, being taken from me; but, even had I been in possession of the power to restore her again to the world, the scene before us would have been sufficient to erase the very wish to keep her an hour longer from the possession of that happy and exalted state of existence into which she was just about to enter, and of which she already enjoyed such a sweet and delightful foretaste. "The house of mourning" was now literally turned into "the house of joy;" every tear was now wiped away, and only one feeling of joy and gratitude filled every bosom present; and as we gazed on the happy spectacle before us, on the eye which beamed with such hallowed delight, and calmly awaited the arrival of the solemn moment, the emotions of our hearts were more like those which pervade the breasts of the guests of a marriage-supper, than of those who were surrounding the death-bed, and taking the last farewell of a dearly-beloved friend: indeed it was impossible, with such a picture before us, to be otherwise. The only regret which seemed to exist was, that the number who were thus to witness a practical testimony to the truth of God's word was not greater: that the doubtful was not there, that he might be confirmed; the man of pleasure, that he might know where true happiness was to be found; the careless, that he might be aroused; the scoffer, that he might tremble; and the infidel, that he might be confounded.

After another brief pause, she requested me to come forward, and, before our final separation, to kiss her. This was the last sad signal that our short and happy union here was now for ever to be dissolved: to human nature it was a trying moment; and as I complied with this last request, she warmly and affectionately repeated, "Again," and "Once more, again," and clasped my hand, while, through the loving, lingering look, she whispered, Farewell, farewell! But although she was now parting with one who fondly loved her, she was going away to meet with Him who "*so* loved" her that he gave up his life as a ransom for her, and from whom she would never, never be separated.

> "A hope so great and so divine,
> May trials well endure."

She also requested the others who were present, slowly naming each of them, one by one to come forward, as she mentioned their names respectively, and to kiss her now cold and icy lips. After this request had been complied with, she desired us, naming each of us again, and in the same order, to come near and take hold of her hand, apparently intending her hand to continue to be joined with ours until death should unloose them. She looked calmly and silently on, until we were all placed in such a position as to be able conveniently to comply with the particulars of her request. After arranging ourselves on each side of the couch on which she lay, and taking hold of her hand in the way she desired, she kept silence for a moment or two, and then said, slowly and sweetly, but in a firm tone of voice, and laying an emphasis on the word "now," "I think I am *now* going to die; but do not weep for me, for I am happy, happy, happy!" And now, perhaps one of the most solemn and sublime spectacles that could pass before the vision of a human being, was witnessed by those who stood around her dying pillow, and one which was calculated not only to establish in the mind of the most sceptical the blessed reality of the religion of Jesus Christ, but to convince the most rigid materialist of the immortal nature of the human soul, for whose present and eternal welfare that religion has been revealed to man. On the one hand, death sat in awful stillness on her pale and marbled countenance, as if unwilling to disturb the sweetness and serenity that were reposing there; and on the other, immortality beamed through the peace, the joy, and the bright intelligence of her eye: here a body, mortal, corrupt, and sinking down to earth; there a soul, deathless, sanctified, and rising up to heaven; the grave opening for the one, the gates of glory for the other: the one unbosoming its immortality, and putting on the dark and dreary mantle of death, purchased by sin; the other flinging aside its earthly habiliments, and gathering around it the white and shining robes of immortal glory, provided by Jesus Christ.

She looked and appeared to feel as if the rising majesty of her immortal nature was calmly smiling at death and the grave, and unwilling to permit her longer to recognize even her own body as part and portion of herself, or to be associated with any thing short of heaven and immortality. Thus waiting in the most perfect consciousness the joyful blast of the jubilee trumpet, the note of ransom to her yet earth-bound spirit, and standing in the very gateway between time and eternity—between earth and heaven—she gently raised her eyes, with a holy and hallowed gaze, towards heaven, when the new Jerusalem appeared to burst on her view, and with a joyful voice she calmly and slowly exclaimed, "Oh, yonder he is, yonder he is! Oh, do you not see him, do you not see him? yonder he is, waiting with open arms to receive me! Oh, could you see what I now see—cherubim and seraphim surrounding the throne, crying and singing Hallelujah, hallelujah, hallelujah to the Lamb who was slain. Oh, yonder he is, yonder he is! Do you not see him, do you not see him?" and again raising her sinking voice, she named me, and directing my attention upward with the finger of her unoccupied hand, again said, "Do you not see him? look, yonder he is, yonder he is!"

After giving utterance to these extraordinary expressions, which she did with a coolness and apparently under a consciousness of the reality of what she referred to, that, without venturing to express any opinion, I may say produced at least an impression upon our minds which will probably never be effaced, she now appeared to feel as if her sinking strength would not permit her again to open her lips; and, still having hold of her hand in the way she had previously desired, we now stood in deep silence, waiting in breathless suspense the arrival of the solemn moment. Observing us in this state of suspense, Mrs. Little broke the general silence, and in that cool and collected manner which she had always hitherto manifested, quietly remarked, "Perhaps it is not going to be just so *very* quick;" the peculiar emphasis she laid on the word "very" intimating that she perceived by our silence and looks that we were in momentary expectation of the approaching change. After another short pause, she calmly said, "Aunt, what time of the day is it just now ?" when Mrs. Cumming informed her that it was just twelve o'clock. From her very significant look and manner when putting this question, her aunt was under the impression that she intended to follow it up with some remarks, but was prevented doing so by the want of physical strength to enable her to give utterance to her sentiments.

At this moment the sun of nature shone out from behind a cloud, illuming with his cheering beams the chamber of death, and revealing more vividly to our gaze the calm and happy features of a redeemed sinner, stepping into eternity under the noontide blaze of the Sun of righteousness. Another brief pause having occurred, she asked for a little cold water. Her articulation was now somewhat difficult, but she still retained full possession of all her mental faculties; and as Mrs. Cumming placed the water to her mouth, she opened her lips and composedly sipped it from the spoon, appearing as conscious and calm as any one present. The spoon, however, was just withdrawn from her lips, and the last sip of water passed down, when, lifting her eyes upward and casting a holy gaze to heaven, she calmly and sweetly looked for a moment—and now her eye is fixed, her heaving bosom gently sinks to rest, the soft breath ceases to fan the half-formed smile still lingering on her lip: no struggle, no pain; a babe-like sweetness sits on her pale features; all is tranquil, all is still: she sleeps—it is the sleep of death! Thus she died—thus she sped away, far beyond the reach of woe, to the realms of eternal glory—away to receive her immortal crown, and to swell the songs of the redeemed around the throne, with God for her father, Christ for her brother, angels for her companions, heaven for her dwelling-place, and eternity for her lifetime.

We were thus left alone, gazing on each other, in silent wonder, at the triumphant scene just witnessed; and, before a word was exchanged, we all united in thanksgiving to God for the extraordinary manifestation of his love which he had just made to pass before us.

We required no longer to pray for her who was formerly so often the subject of our petitions. Happy woman! she was now already robed in spotless white, with a crown of glory on her brow, and triumphantly waving her palm of victory, amid the joyful hallelujahs of the redeemed in heaven, where death and suffering, where sorrow and sighing, have for ever fled away. Having followed her with the eye of our mind away to the upper sanctuary, and left her disappearing amid the shining throng, within the golden gates of the new Jerusalem, the beautiful but lifeless form which she had left behind, now shrouded in the deep tranquillity of death and stretched before us, led us to feel anew the solemn warning, "Prepare to meet thy God:" "Be thou also ready;" "for there is no work, nor device, nor knowledge, nor wisdom, in the grave, whither thou goest;" and to see, in all its truthfulness, that "all flesh is grass." The beloved one whose lifeless body lay before us, was the youngest of the company; but eighteen years she had sojourned on earth, and only thirteen short but happy months had winged their flight since the same two hands which death had just for ever separated, were joined by the most endearing tie on earth: thirteen short months before, she stood by the side of him from whom she had just taken the last farewell, a lovely and blooming bride of seventeen, arrayed in her wedding garments; now she lay before him a pale, cold, and lifeless corpse, robed in the dreary grave sheet: the dark and cheerful eye, which beamed so brightly only a few weeks before, was now for ever shut in death. And now he listens for the sound of that voice which was wont to fall so sweetly on his ear; but all is silent as the grave: he gazes round, and there her empty chair meets his eye; here lies her needle, threaded with her own hand, and stuck in her unfinished seam; there the sacred spot where, in secret, she was wont to pour out her soul to her Father in heaven, lonely and deserted; and here lies her Bible, with the careful mark at the verse which last she read. Truly we realized "the vanity of all things here below," and felt that

"Whate'er we fondly call our own
Belongs to heaven's great Lord;
The blessings lent us for a day,
Are soon to be restored.

'Tis God that lifts our comforts high,
  Or sinks them in the grave;
He gives—and when he takes away,
  He takes but what he gave."

In the evening, a meeting for thanksgiving to God for his gracious dealings to the departed—for having led her by his Holy Spirit to "the Lamb of God who taketh away the sin of the world," supported her under her long and severe affliction, and enabled her to die a blessed testimony to "the truth as it is in Jesus," was held by a few of our Christian friends in the room adjoining "the chamber of death." It was a happy and delightful meeting, and truly the Holy Spirit, the Comforter, was in the midst of us; the house of mourning was in reality felt to be "the house of joy." Some of Mrs. Little's favorite hymns were sung; and as our hearts and voices were blending in praise

"To Him who loved the souls of men,
  And washed us in his blood,"

we thought of her who was no longer with us, as being engaged at the same time in singing some sweet "song of Zion," with the company of the redeemed in heaven. Some of those present had many a time before met in sweet fellowship with Mrs. Little in the same apartment in which we were now assembled, to sing praises to God and the Lamb who was slain, to talk to each other about their eternal peace, to pray with and for each other, for believers of every name, for the unconverted, and for the speedy arrival of that time when "the earth shall be full of the knowledge of the Lord, as the waters cover the sea."

These meetings, intended for promoting the growth in grace and personal sanctification of the children of God who there assembled, had always afforded Mrs. Little great spiritual enjoyment. Next to her secret fellowship with God, fellowship with God's redeemed children on earth yielded her the most delight. Now, however, she was absent; her chair was empty; her voice was missing in the song of praise; and, as the cold, unbreathing, unconscious form, sleeping in death in the adjoining room, intimated in solemn accents that she would be absent still, that her chair would be vacant still, and that her voice would be silent still, we only realized more sweetly that she had then begun the happier and never-ending fellowship with the saints in glory; that her absence from us was her presence with Jesus, and that her silence in our weak song of praise, was the sound of her voice in the lofty hallelujahs of the ransomed above.

On the following Wednesday, Mrs. Little's mortal remains were conveyed to Sight-hill Cemetery, in the northern suburbs of Glasgow, and there deposited in the dark and silent tomb, by the side of her "dear Jane," who had ten days "gone to glory before her," there to slumber till the morning of the resurrection.

"When the last trumpet's awful voice
This rending earth shall shake;
When opening graves shall yield their charge,
And dust to life awake;
Those bodies that corrupted fell,
Shall incorrupted rise;
And mortal forms shall spring to life,
Immortal, in the skies."

Thus, at the age of eighteen, Mrs. Little's earthly pilgrimage for ever terminated; and as we left the dreary habitations of the dead, and looked back amid the tombstones on the silent, new-made mound of earth which appeared in the distance, our minds involuntarily exclaimed within us,

"Few are thy days, and full of woe,
O man, of woman born;
Thy doom is written: 'Dust thou art,
And shalt to dust return!'"

And yet, though frail human nature and human affections will thus sometimes wander back and gaze into her silent resting-place, our contemplations cannot linger long around her tomb: she is not there; upward, on the finished work of Jesus, she was borne away to heaven; and the mind, looking through the revealed truth of the God "who cannot lie," can discover her nowhere but among the blessed company of the redeemed, who are "clothed in robes made white in the blood of the Lamb," singing hallelujah, hallelujah to him who was slain; for "these things have I written unto you that believe on the name of the Son of God, that ye may know that ye have eternal life." "Blessed are the dead who die in the Lord," for henceforth they are "heirs of God and joint-heirs of Jesus Christ." Such glorious truths, standing in the view of the bereaved and forlorn soul, make such a parting with a dear friend only sweet and delightful, and leave no room for one breathing of regret:

Oh no, complain we cannot, murmur we cannot; weep, we may, but only tears of joy.

On the succeeding Sabbath, Mrs. Little's funeral-sermon was preached by Mr. Pullar, her pastor, in North-Albion-street chapel, to a crowded and deeply-affected audience, from the words which had been chosen by herself for the occasion, namely, "Believe in the Lord Jesus Christ, and thou shalt be saved;" and it will be interesting and pleasing to the converted reader to be informed, that the sermon was, in the hands of the Spirit, made the instrument of leading at least *one* unconverted sinner to "believe in the Lord Jesus Christ," and to rejoice in the liberty of the gospel.

A short time after Mrs. Little's death, Mrs. Cumming of Selkirk, who has been frequently alluded to in these pages, forwarded to the writer a manuscript written by Mrs. Little, and entitled "A Friend," which was discovered in a drawer used by her when residing with her uncle's family in Selkirk; a copy of which is annexed, on account of the remarkable confirmation in Mrs. Little's own after-experience, of the important truths it contains and so clearly illustrates; but more especially for the benefit of the unconverted reader, for whom chiefly these pages are written. The manuscript is written on two sheets of letter-paper, and appears to have been intended either to be sent to some friend or acquaintance of Mrs. Little, or to be retained by her as a faithful representation of the opinion of her own mind, regarding the "Friend" it alludes to; the latter was most probably the case.

"A FRIEND.

"Do you want a friend, powerful to protect you, rich to supply your wants, kind to sympathize with you, affectionate to feel for you, wise to guide you—a friend that sticketh closer than a brother; one to whom you can go at all times, at all seasons, under all circumstances; one to whom you can open all your heart; one who is able to satisfy your craving desire for happiness, who can assist you when all other friends fail, who can support you in your last agonies, and walk with you through the dark valley of the shadow of death; one whose influence and power extends beyond the grave, who is able to save you and give you a place among the sons of God?

"Reader, as you are a lost and perishing sinner, if you desire such a friend, let me tell you to your joy that I know of one who is not only all this, but who is far more valuable—far more excellent—far more desirable, than all that this description implies; his name is "Jesus." He is powerful to protect you, for he is the Son of the living God: he is rich to supply you, for he is God the all-sufficient; in him are all the treasures of wisdom and knowledge. Are you, in a spiritual sense, poor, and wretched, and miserable, and blind, and naked? he will give you his Holy Spirit; and when you are oppressed under a sense of your sinfulness, the Comforter will give you such confidence in the declaration, that 'the blood of Jesus Christ his Son cleanseth us from all sin,' as shall bring peace to your soul.

"Whatever temporal things you may want, this kind friend is no less able than willing to supply, if they are suitable for you. Do you want one to sympathize with you? Seek Jesus for your friend, and trust in what he has done and suffered for you, believe in the efficacy of his atoning blood, and you will find that there can be no friend more sympathetic than he. He is also affectionate to feel for you—that love which brought him from the skies he still retains, nor is its warmth diminished; he is wise to guide you, he knows all your circumstances, your difficulties, and your dangers; he is the friend that sticketh closer than a brother; he will bear with your weakness with more than a brother's forbearance; he is not confined to any place, so that wherever you are you may have access to him—no change of circumstances alters his affection; he will befriend you in sickness as well as in health, in old age as well as in youth, in adversity as well as in prosperity; he is one to whom you can give all your heart, for he has given you such amazing proofs of his love that you cannot doubt his affection. Think of God as God incarnate—God in human flesh—dying for your sins, that you might not perish, but have everlasting life, and you cannot but be willing to pour out your heart before him, and to confide in his love. O take him for your friend, and then you will perceive how worthy he is of your tenderest affections.

"Reader, you thirst for happiness: in vain do you seek for it in earthly enjoyments; your desires after happiness are so extensive, that nothing can satisfy them but the enjoyment of God. Take Jesus for your friend, and he will make you completely happy. A time is fast approaching when earthly friends cannot aid you; they cannot save you from the hour of death—they cannot support you in your last moments, nor accompany you through the dark valley of the shadow of death; but the friend now pointed out, the blessed Jesus, can comfort and support when all other friends can render you no assistance; he can receive your parting spirit, convey you safely through the dark shades of death, and bring you to everlasting happiness. He died for your sins: believe in him, trust in what he has done and suffered, and you shall be delivered from the blackness of darkness for ever and ever; for 'God so loved the world that he gave his only begotten Son, that whosoever believeth in him should not perish, but have everlasting life.'"

Such is a brief and simple history of Mrs. Little's Christian experience here below, and of its cheering and triumphant termination. The narrative is not intended to represent the history of the individual, but only of the Christian; it is an account, not of human merit, but of divine grace: and the desired results of its perusal are not to occupy the remembrance of the reader with the humble subject of its pages, who was only a poor sinful worm of the dust—not to detain his mental vision with circumstances which may only excite his interest and confer upon him no real practical benefit; but under the guidance of the Holy Spirit, to establish in his bosom "peace with God through our Lord Jesus Christ," and to leave his soul gazing upward to a God "well pleased," and to a broken law "satisfied" with the work of Jesus for his sins. The task of furnishing such a narrative has, to the writer, been productive of not a few painful reminiscences; and to these its publication will add a feeling of deep regret, if its perusal should contribute to any other result than the one referred to. To seek, through the narrative, the bestowal of any thing like merit or praise on the subject of its pages, would only be to insult her memory, and the God and Saviour of her soul. There is no merit in being a Christian; Christianity, from first to last, is a system of total dependence on the merits of another. For all that she was, therefore, for all that she now is, and will continue throughout eternity to be, the honor and the merit are due to Him alone; and could her voice be now heard from her high and holy habitation, it would be exclaiming, "Not unto me, not unto me, but to God be all the glory."

As the exhibition of a *consequence*, in connection with practical chemistry or natural philosophy, is intended by the lecturer to direct back the mind of his pupil to the *cause* which produced it, so the great object of these pages is to lead the mind of the unconverted reader into a practical contact with only one great and inconceivably important truth, the *knowledge* of which will leave in his possession a treasure, whose value is so great that the power of the human mind cannot sum it up; the cost of which was so immense, that to estimate its amount baffles all calculation. And what is that which is so valuable, so costly? Is it some vast mine of the finest gold? No; the Peruvian treasures would only dim its lustre. Is it the possession of a crown and kingdom? No; these would only sully its beauty and glory. Is it the inheritance of the world itself? Oh, no; ten thousand worlds cannot purchase it. God calls it "eternal life." And what did it cost? Calvary replies, "*The life of Jesus Christ his Son and equal.*" But although advantage has been taken of those openings and avenues which occasionally presented themselves by the way, of directing the attention of the inquiring reader to a view of that great truth, perhaps the eye of his mind has been so occupied by its fruits and its foliage, as he travelled along, that he may not yet have seen, or seen but dimly and sideways, the *source* from which all their sweetness proceeded. If such be the case, he is still unsaved, unhappy—a cloud of fear still envelopes his weary and sin-laden soul; and he is therefore invited now to turn his mind away from all the circumstances which may have occupied his attention in the foregoing narrative, and to fix his gaze on that truth, the perception of which, on his part, will bring salvation to his soul, fill his mind with hallowed joy, and sweep away all his fears.

www.ingramcontent.com/pod-product-compliance
Lightning Source LLC
LaVergne TN
LVHW021418110826
845150LV00007B/1978

* 9 7 8 1 4 2 5 5 0 9 7 8 1 *